T0338112

Extracting Appalachia

EXTRACTING APPALACHIA

**Images of
the Consolidation
Coal Company,
1910–1945**

Geoffrey L. Buckley

OHIO UNIVERSITY PRESS
Athens

Ohio University Press, Athens, Ohio 45701
© 2004 by Geoffrey L. Buckley

Ohio University Press books are printed on acid-free paper ⊗ ™

12 11 10 09 08 07 06 05 04   5 4 3 2 1

Cover art: "Railroad depot at Fleming, Kentucky"; *Frontispiece:* "No. 212 opening 1916," from Smithsonian Institution, National Museum of American History, Consolidation Coal Company Photgraphs.

Library of Congress Cataloging-in-Publication Data

Buckley, Geoffrey L., 1965-
    Extracting Appalachia : images of the Consolidation Coal Company,
1910-1945 / Geoffrey L. Buckley.
        p. cm.
    Includes bibliographical references and index.
    ISBN 0-8214-1555-7 (cloth : alk. paper) – ISBN 0-8214-1556-5 (pbk. : alk. paper)
        1. Consolidation Coal Company–History. 2. Consolidation Coal
Company–Pictorial works. 3. Coal mines and mining–Appalachian
Region–History. 4. Coal mines and mining–Appalachian
Region–Pictorial works. 5. Appalachian Region–Pictorial works. I.
Title: Images of the Consolidation Coal Company, 1910-1945. II. Title.
TN805.Z6 B83 2004
338.4'7622334'0974022–dc22

                                                2003022073

For Ingrid and Peter

Contents

Acknowledgments

A great many people helped me bring this project to a successful conclusion. First and foremost, I would like to thank the editorial staff at Ohio University for their guidance and professionalism. I am especially grateful to Gillian Berchowitz, who planted the seed and nurtured it from the start; David Sanders, whose financial and intellectual support were invaluable; Nancy Basmajian, who shepherded the project through its final stages; Bob Furnish, who helped me say what I meant to say all along; and Sharon Rose, who offered advice at various stages of the process.

I owe a great debt of gratitude to several reviewers, all of whom gave generously of their time. I am particularly indebted to Richard Francaviglia and William Wyckoff, whose encouragement and critical comments improved the manuscript considerably. I am also fortunate to have had Lary Dilsaver, Ronald Lewis, and Joan Schwartz offer their criticism of individual chapters. At Ohio University, Leslie Flemming, Nancy Bain, Howard Dewald, and Roxanne Malé-Brune supported my efforts with release time and special funding.

Numerous archivists, curators, and specialized staff assisted me along the way. Peter Liebhold, Betsy Robinson, and David Burgevin provided me with access to the Smithsonian Institution's "hidden treasures" and made it possible for me to acquire the images that are featured in this book. Betty Van Newkirk gave me free range of the Frostburg Museum archives and entrusted me with her entire collection of CCC *Mutual Monthly Magazines*, a gesture of kindness and generosity I will not soon forget. George Bain and Patricia Smith-Hunt made it possible for me to obtain a microfilm copy of the magazines for Ohio University. Lanna and Charles Dixon introduced me to the wonderful assortment of archival materials housed at the David A. Zegeer Coal-Railroad Museum in Jenkins, Kentucky. I must also tip my hat to the dedicated librarians at the Maryland Historical

Society, West Virginia University, and the University of Maryland for their patience and assistance.

Although I am a geographer by training, I am no cartographer. All credit for the map in the introduction goes to Hugh Bloemer and Jesse Glasscock. Undergraduate assistants Kasey Snyder, Jillian Buckholz, and Katie Reeves carried out several data searches and assisted with other tasks. Fellow Athenians Gifford Doxsee, Bill Kaldis, Sigmund Kozma, Glenn Ray, Reid Sinclair, and Jack Wright contributed in various ways, as did my good friend Eric Wagner, who put up with much talk about photographs he had never seen. Most of all, I would like to thank my wife, Alexandra, and my two children, Ingrid and Peter. Every day you bring joy and wonder to my life.

A Remarkable Collection

The past is what you remember, imagine you remember, convince
yourself you remember, or pretend to remember.

—Harold Pinter

A photograph, whilst recording what has been seen, always and
by its nature refers to what is not seen.

—John Berger

While conducting research in support of a doctoral disser-
tation several years ago at the Smithsonian Institution's National
Museum of American History in Washington, D.C., it was my good fortune to stumble upon a truly remarkable collection of coal-mining photographs. Numbering close to four thousand in all and covering an
impressive range of topics, the collection had formerly belonged to the
powerful Consolidation Coal Company. Some of the photos show commonplace mining features. Others were far less prosaic: deforested hillsides, locomotive wrecks, striking workers, mine accident fatalities, and
miners whose fingers and limbs appeared to be getting severed or crushed
by heavy machinery. Images that plainly showed the separate status of
African American miners and their families were particularly provocative.

According to the captions and album labels, most of the pictures in
the coal company's archive were taken during the first half of the twentieth century. By far the greatest number were taken in Kentucky and West
Virginia. Given my topic—the environmental impacts of coal mining in
western Maryland—it was my intention to focus specifically on those
images that would directly support my research. As I rummaged through

cardboard boxes and thumbed the pages of leather-bound albums, however, I could not help but be drawn in by the entire collection. Who took these pictures? Why were they made? How were they used? Of only one thing could I be certain—I had another research project waiting in the wings.[1]

Uncovering the Past

Anyone who has ever studied people or events of the past knows the caveats attached to such work. A few years ago historian William Cronon remarked that conducting historical research was akin to telling "stories about stories." Put another way, because scholars in the present are unable to truly experience the past, their historical curiosities must be satisfied by relying on a variety of problematic and incomplete data sets. As one might expect, the less reliable the data are, the more diminished is the researcher's ability to interpret the past. According to geographer David Lowenthal, we also must bear in mind that the past can never be known or understood like the present and that there exists no absolute truth waiting to be uncovered. To make matters worse, our ability to understand the past is hindered by hindsight; that is, more is known about past events and circumstances than people of the past could ever have known at the time. That survivals from the past are always scattered, incomplete, and sometimes contradictory should not exclude the study of past places from the researcher's agenda, however. Rather, a focus on available factual evidence and, in the words of geographer Cole Harris, an "unremitting effort to be accurate" should combine to provide an informed interpretation of past places and processes.[2]

While photographs offer us certain unique opportunities when it comes to "knowing" the past, they also present us with unique challenges. While much of what is contained in the photos that I studied would have been familiar to anyone associated with Consol's operations at the time, to present-day observers the photos would not—indeed they could not—strike the same chord. Perusing the collection at the museum one day, I recalled a passage from Peirce Lewis's chapter in a well-worn copy of Donald Meinig's *Interpretation of Ordinary Landscapes:*

> Architectural historians publish books full of handsome photographs of "important buildings," artfully composed so that the viewer will not see the "less important" building next door, much

less the telephone wires overhead or the gas station across the street. The "important building" is disembodied, as if on an architect's easel in a windowless studio somewhere. . . . So it is with houses and barns and lawns and sidewalks and any other "item" in the landscape: to make sense of them, one must observe them in context.

And so it is with the images in the Consolidation Coal Company archive. To make any sense of them at all, they must be situated in both historical and spatial context. This is particularly important given that they were company photographs taken to satisfy contemporary company needs. To interpret them in any other way—to view them as "neutral" windows on the past for instance—would be confusing at best and at worst, misleading.[3]

The Rise of an Industry Giant

First and foremost, we must remember that all the photographs in the Smithsonian collection exist because of coal or, more precisely, because of our demand for coal. Referring to the tremendous increase in the scale of mining operations that characterized the late nineteenth and early twentieth centuries in the United States, geographer Richard V. Francaviglia writes that this demand for minerals "was spurred by a rapidly growing population that consumed more natural materials as a consumer-oriented society was created; which is to say that our mining landscapes are a reflection of our growing affluence as a nation." It follows then that the mining landscapes we create today are a reflection of our continued demand for and dependence on natural materials, as well as our desire to maintain a lifestyle based on high energy inputs. At a time when the coal industry's future is the subject of spirited debate, particularly in places where controversial techniques such as mountaintop removal are being challenged by both environmentalists and local residents, we would do well to remind ourselves of a time when coal satisfied the lion's share of our energy needs and our tolerance for environmental destruction was much higher than it is today.[4]

It would be difficult to exaggerate the importance of coal in fueling America's industrial revolution. A cursory glance at production figures for the nineteenth century illustrates this point well. Between 1800 and 1832 production of coal in the United States increased from a mere hundred

Fig. I.1. "Block of Fairmont Coal." This photograph appeared in the CCC *Mutual Monthly Magazine*, April 1924, with the following caption: "Block of coal recently taken from Mine No. 22, W. Va., for shipment to Italy, where it will be placed on exhibition. This is one of the largest blocks of coal ever removed from a West Virginia mine. It is 8 ft. 6 in. high by 4 ft. 6 in. wide by 4 ft. 6 in. thick and weighs approximately 6½ tons."

thousand tons to over one million tons per year. By 1851 production had soared to 10 million tons, and by 1860 the figure stood at 20 million tons. The advent of coal-burning locomotives led to the extraction of 110 million tons in 1885 and 243 million tons in 1900, by which time the United States had become the world's leading producer. To put it bluntly, as historian Duane A. Smith has done, "Without mining—from coal to iron to gold—the United States could not have emerged as a world power by the turn of the century, nor could it have successfully launched its international career of the twentieth century." Historically, Appalachia's coalfields contributed mightily to America's emergence as an industrial power (fig. I.1).⁵

The story of the Consolidation Coal Company, with which we are chiefly concerned, closely mirrors that of the coal industry in general. It is the story of the rise to prominence of one of America's industrial giants (fig. I.2). From its modest beginnings in western Maryland's Georges Creek valley in the 1860s to its emergence as the largest producer of bituminous coal in the United States in 1926, Consolidation Coal played a leading role in transforming America into an industrial power. While much scholarly attention has been directed toward Appalachia over the years, relatively little has focused on coal-mining landscapes and, more specifically, on the pivotal role industry titans like Consolidation Coal played in creating, shaping, and reshaping those landscapes. It seems that little has changed in the ten years since Margaret Mulrooney declared that "little attention has been given to the role of bituminous coal towns in determining the physical and social character" of our coal-mining regions. And yet these communities served as the focal points of the coal industry throughout much of this period:

Dependent upon natural geography and geology for their existence, these communities shaped not only the physical landscape but also the cultural identity of the region. . . . The region has historically been considered to have the most important deposits of coal in the United States. Of these states, Pennsylvania was consistently ranked as the leading producer of both bituminous and anthracite coal between 1880 and 1930. The Appalachian region produced 92 percent of the total amount of coal mined in the United States in 1925. Pennsylvania, alone, contributed about one-third.

Richard Francaviglia also acknowledged this lack of attention: "most of our mining history sites focus on metals: very few interpret coal mining, which is equally important, but less romantic in that it did not tend to make the individual prospector rich."[6]

Lack of romance notwithstanding, numerous sources are available to aid us in the reconstruction and interpretation of coal-mining landscapes. Clearly, the Smithsonian's photo archive of the Consolidation Coal Company is one of them. Between the end of the first decade of the twentieth century and the close of the Second World War, thousands of photographs were taken of coal company activities, property, and equipment in several states. Collectively, they yield a glimpse of life and labor in central Appalachia's coalfields. More specifically, they allow us to follow closely the construction and development of mines and company towns; to

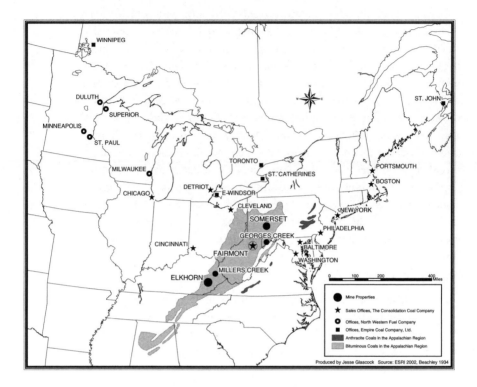

Fig. I.2. Location of mine properties and offices of the Consolidation Coal Company (after Beachley 1934).

inspect the work of miners; to track the technological advances that revolutionized the industry; to observe conditions in and around the mines and mining communities; and to speculate on social and cultural aspects of coal town life. Similarly, scenes of environmental devastation tell us much about the values and priorities that guided past use of natural resources.[7]

Another valuable source is the coal company periodical. According to historian John C. Hennen, "employee magazines" came into popular use during the early years of the twentieth century and were commonly used by coal companies to influence worker behavior and output:

> The first such publications appeared in 1907 and proliferated dramatically between 1915 and 1920, when over four hundred companies published monthly or bimonthly journals. Designed to convince employees that the company was concerned about their individual happiness, goals, and successes, employee magazines sought to bind worker to employer in a consciousness of cooperation, trust, and affirmation of probusiness views of industrial relations. . . . The ideological currents of industrial Americanization, scientific management, anti-unionism, and the American Plan are well-defined in one of the most prominent coal industry employee magazines, the *Consolidation Coal Company Mutual Monthly*.

Between 1918 and 1928, approximately eleven thousand copies of the *CCC Mutual Monthly* were published monthly, and later, bimonthly, by the company's Employment Relations Department. In addition to regular features, such as the health and safety column and the "company editorial," the *Mutual Monthly* carried news from mining communities in each of the company's divisions. Lodge meetings, announcements of various men's and women's clubs, ball games and tournaments, dances and box socials, birth announcements and death notices, weddings and anniversaries, job changes, religious revivals and Chautauquas, school news, first-aid meetings, local weather conditions, society gossip, and holiday celebrations—all were covered in the pages of the magazine. If there were newcomers to town or if someone purchased a new car, radio, or Victrola or had a particularly successful hunting or fishing trip, it was covered in the magazine. Most important for our purposes, the *CCC Mutual Monthly* served as a key outlet for many of the photographs in the Smithsonian collection, as well as for other images submitted to the magazine's editors. That a single image could be reproduced eleven thousand times and distributed to far-flung mining communities in several states speaks to the hidden power of the photograph to deliver messages on behalf of the company.[8]

As students of American economic history well know, coal's ascendancy and domination of energy markets was not destined to last. By the 1920s, it was obvious that all was not well with the coal industry. As one source put it in 1976:

> From 1890 to the First World War, the coal industry resisted the considerable efforts of its operators to bring order to what was widely regarded, by government officials and mine workers as well as operators, as an excessively competitive industry. . . . This interstate competition reflected the wide availability of coal and the labor to mine it, the relatively low capital requirements for its development, and the ease with which one coal (or an alternative energy source) could be substituted for another. The result was a low-profit industry with chronic and growing excess capacity and an extremely low level of concentration.

Here again, the *Mutual Monthly* was on hand to provide updates on mine openings and closings, to supply information on coal car availability, and to furnish readers with the company's or coal industry's perspective on everything from the importance of personal hygiene to the evils of union membership. As we shall see later, the photographs in the museum collection offer no indication of the economic hard times that had settled in by the 1920s. This was simply not a message the coal company wished to broadcast to a wider audience, at least not through the medium of photographs.[9]

The Allure of Photographs

Rarely do we "receive" a photograph without any strings attached. Because of the many steps involved in their production and the manner in which they are packaged, we are usually forced, consciously or unconsciously, to interpret photographs at some level. If photos are examined uncritically and out of historical context, accurate interpretation may prove elusive. As Joan M. Schwartz, senior photography specialist at the National Archives of Canada, recently put it, images are not "found" but constructed. Therefore, we must rethink the nature, production and purpose of photographs as documents in order to achieve a contextual understanding of their use by government, business, and individuals to convey government policy, communicate corporate ideology, construct national identity, shape collective memory, establish symbolic space, and define concepts of self and the cultural Other . . . photographs are documents, created by a will, for a purpose, to convey a message to an audience. To understand them as the product of actions and transactions, either bureaucratic or socio-cultural, we must return them to the action in which they participated. It is their functional context that transforms photographic images into archival documents.

All too often we assume photographs to be objective recorders of reality, "a mechanical and therefore neutral means of documentation." Art critic John Berger explains that nothing could be further from the truth:

Photographs bear witness to a human choice being exercised in a given situation. A photograph is a result of the photographer's decision that it is worth recording that this particular event or this particular object has been seen. If everything that existed were continually being photographed, every photograph would become meaningless. A photograph celebrates neither the event itself nor the faculty of sight in itself. A photograph is already a message about the event it records. The urgency of this message is not entirely dependent on the urgency of the event, but neither can it be entirely independent from it.

"At its simplest," writes Berger, "the message, decoded, means: *I have decided that seeing this is worth recording.*"[10]

Although the idea runs counter to what many of us instinctively believe, Schwartz cautions that optical precision is no guarantee of documentary neutrality. Perhaps equally inimical, we must recognize that the photograph itself is a complex document. It is "a representation willed into existence for a purpose and mediated by the persons concurring in its formation. Its message is embedded in the visual transcription of facts, but emerges only in functional context." Both Berger and Schwartz submit that photographic production is a complex process, involving more than a photographer and a subject. It is a process mediated by editors and writers, sponsored oftentimes by governments or businesses, and influenced in

Fig. I.3. "Motor truck on way to Hellier, Sept. 16, 1911."

many and varied ways by numerous other participants. Schwartz also argues that the "spontaneity" of photographic documentation, especially with respect to historic prints, is largely myth: "The need to transport cumbersome equipment and chemicals, and the requirement to prepare negatives or create artificial lighting, involved a decision to document separate from the act of documenting. . . . Commissions and assignments for government, business, or newspapers continue to make photography a deliberate and premeditated act."[11]

How then might we analyze the photograph in figure I.3? Thanks to the caption we are able to date the picture accurately; that is, assuming the caption is correct. Even without the caption, the make and model of the vehicle, as well as the clothing of the vehicle's occupants, provide us with valuable clues concerning the date. Similarly, the sign displayed in the image permits us to identify the owner of the truck and place the scene geographically. The condition of the road and the fact that the truck requires chains appears to validate the claim that it is "the first motor truck" (or at least one of the first) in Letcher County, Kentucky. Finally, the fence in the background suggests a property line of some sort, while its style indicates an abundance of timber in the immediate area. What more can we say about the image? Perhaps we could say that it commemorates the arrival of "modern" transportation to a rural area. Or that it celebrates the coming of a new industrial age to the Southern mountains. Then again, we might conclude that it immortalizes the first stage of an era of environmental destruction. Or that it symbolizes the end of a particular way of life for many of the region's residents. In truth, without additional information, we cannot say much more.

As is so often the case when one begins to explore a new topic, we are left at the outset with more questions than answers. Why did the company elect to have this particular photograph made? What information was the company attempting to communicate? How did company officials intend to use the image? What was the company trying to accomplish in this part of Kentucky? To answer these and many other questions necessarily requires that we treat this image and all the others in the collection as texts that can be read and studied and, further, that we place them in their proper historical context, a process that unfolds over the course of the next several chapters.

The period when the Consolidation Coal photographs were taken was an extraordinary one for the coal industry. It was a period of economic prosperity for many coal operators and investors. A period marked by great technological advances and tremendous expansion of operations. A period that saw Consolidation Coal become the country's largest producer of bituminous coal. Company-sponsored histories, promotional literature, and photographs published over the past century clearly reflect the pride Consolidation has taken in this storied past. Just as cultural anthropologist Allen Batteau, in reference to the literature of coal-mining development, once marveled at "how the dull prose of engineering takes off for rhapsodic heights when discussing the pioneering and progressive role of the coal industry in central Appalachia," we shall see how Consol's glowing interpretation of its own past compares with the interpretations others have forwarded. Truth be told, this was also a period that brought financial ruin to many associated with the coal industry. A period of struggle between management and labor. A period marred by social strife and environmental devastation. Indeed, at the other end of the spectrum, individuals not tied to the industry in some way have cast the coal companies—Consolidation Coal included—in an altogether different light.[12]

My purpose here is not to write yet another history of coal mining in Appalachia. That task has been carried out ably by others. Nor is it my intention to excoriate the coal industry for its poor safety record, its abuse of individual liberties, its antiunionism, and its use of heavyhanded tactics during the first three decades of the twentieth century. No doubt these are valid criticisms, even if sometimes we have carried the generalizations too far. At any rate, that too has already been done. And it is certainly not my wish to portray miners as "destroying Huns" and to accuse them of "raping and pillaging" the land. The historical record simply does not support such an allegation. Rather, my purpose is to critically examine the photographs in the Consolidation Coal collection, place them in historical context, and try to understand why they were taken and for whom.[13]

With these goals in mind, I have divided the remainder of the book into six chapters. In chapter 1, I expand on the discussion of photographs already initiated in this introduction. After a brief review of the geographical concept of landscape, including its links to nineteenth-century American lithographs and other forms of visual representation, I survey recent scholarship on photographs to gain a better appreciation for them as historical documents, as opposed to illustrative props. I then touch on some of the ways photographs have been used in the past to promote tourism, win support for political programs, and advance the interests of private industry. Chapter 2 offers a detailed history of the Consolidation Coal Company. Starting with its earliest corporate antecedent, the Maryland Mining Company, I recount the key events in the company's history, as well as the principle people and connections, that allowed it to develop into a major player in the industry, from its incorporation in Maryland in 1860 to its merger with the Pittsburgh Coal Company in 1945.

Chapters 3 through 5 are organized thematically. Chapter 3 focuses specifically on photographs relating to life in the company town. Images of coal towns, company stores, and miners' gardens are featured, as are pictures that provide evidence of the cultural diversity that characterized these carefully planned and tightly controlled communities. In chapter 4, the emphasis shifts to work-related pictures. Images of men at work, mining equipment, and health-and-safety training figure prominently in this section. Here special attention is also devoted to themes not covered to any great extent in the photograph collection, chiefly unions and economic depression. Images of environmental alteration comprise the bulk of those analyzed in chapter 5. In addition to scenes of forest destruction and stream degradation, the company documented the construction of many of their mines and coal-handling facilities. Thus we are left with a remarkable record of "before and after" shots that show the complete environmental transformation that took place in places like eastern Kentucky from the time the company acquired the rights to woodland farms to the point where the development of a mining landscape was well underway.

The final chapter has several functions. In addition to summarizing key points brought out in preceding chapters, it sheds light on the Consol collection by comparing its contents with that of other photographic collections, including portions of the Mary Behner Christopher Collection and the Farm Security Administration file.

A Note on the Photographs

Given the size of the collection, I had to be highly selective when it came to choosing photographs for the book. In making a final determination, I tried to select images that were either unique in terms of content or representative of major themes that run throughout the entire collection. Whenever possible I have provided the original captions, enclosed in quotation marks. In a handful of cases, the photographs were not accompanied by captions, in which case I have done my best to describe them. Unless otherwise noted, all photographs are courtesy of the Smithsonian Institution, National Museum of American History.

Reading Historical Photographs

In sum, landscape is an historic document that tells a story—nay, multiple stories—about the people who created the landscape—and the cultural context in which that landscape was embedded.

—Peirce Lewis

Images are captivating but suspect.

—Yi-Fu Tuan

Photographs have a mesmerizing quality about them. Anyone who has ever perused the pages of a daily newspaper, major news weekly, or popular magazine has experienced firsthand the power of photographs to communicate information and influence public opinion. Indeed, a single provocative image is capable of eliciting a variety of emotional responses from an audience, running the gamut from fear and anger to joy and relief to anguish and horror. In recent years, electronic access to a wide range of news and other sources has served to magnify the effect of these visual stimuli by providing near "real-time" images to a growing population of worldwide web users.[1]

Historical photographs are capable of producing similar reactions. They strike emotional chords that reside deep in our collective subconscious, triggering our ability to recall people, places, and events from the past. A strong reaction may be educed even when relatively little is known about the subject matter captured on film. We often assume that these photographs are objective conveyors of truth, "windows on the past" that allow us to journey through time, visit faraway places, and observe events without actually being there. Unwittingly, we place an abiding faith in the

1

truthfulness of photographs. It is this faith that allows us to travel confidently as "virtual witnesses." The reason for this trust in the veracity of the photograph is simple—for many of us seeing is believing. Cultural geographer Yi-Fu Tuan has pointed out, however, that "Seeing may be believing, but believing is not understanding." In short, if examined uncritically or out of historical context, photographs—regardless of when and where they were taken or by whom—are capable of deceiving us.[2]

Lessons from Landscape Interpretation

As geographer Donald W. Meinig showed us nearly a quarter century ago, the deception may be entirely innocent. In his groundbreaking and seminal work *The Interpretation of Ordinary Landscapes,* Meinig does not focus specifically on photographs per se, but on the broader concept of landscape—an avenue of inquiry particularly germane to the study of photographs:

> It will soon be apparent that even though we gather together and look in the same direction at the same instant, we will not—we cannot—see the same landscape. We may certainly agree that we will see many of the same elements—houses, roads, trees, hills,— in terms of such denotations as number, form, dimension, and color, but such facts take on meaning only through association; they must be fitted together according to some coherent body of ideas. Thus we confront the central problem: any landscape is composed not only of what lies before our eyes but what lies within our heads.

In another chapter in the same volume, Yi-Fu Tuan contends that a landscape cannot be defined by simply itemizing its parts. Rather, the parts serve as "subsidiary clues to an integrated image." Put another way, landscape is "an ordering of reality from different angles." It combines the objective with the subjective, the sociological with the ecological. The result is that people are drawn to different aspects of the same landscape. Their characterizations of the scene—including their feelings about what they see—may be so different as to convince a disinterested third party that he or she is reading descriptions of two entirely different places. And as Peirce F. Lewis informs us, history matters:

> [A] large part of the common American landscape was built by people *in* the past, whose tastes, habits, technology, wealth, and ambi-

tions were different than ours today. Thus, while we live among obsolete artifacts of past times—"old-fashioned houses" and "obsolete cities" and "inefficient transportation" or "bad plumbing"— those objects were not seen to be "inefficient" or silly by the people who made them, or caused them to be made. To understand those objects, we must try to understand the people who built them—our cultural ancestors—in *their* cultural context, not ours.

Suffice it to say that the importance of landscape lies in the fact that the way people view their world at any given point in time provides us with, as geographer Denis Cosgrove once put it, "a vital clue to the way they understand that world and their relationships with it."[3]

Building on Meinig's classic volume, others engaged in landscape analysis—among them Toni Alexander, Denis Cosgrove, James and Nancy Duncan, Deryck Holdsworth, Don Mitchell, Edward Relph, Richard Schein, and Bret Wallach—have reinforced the notion that landscape interpretation requires us to focus on that which is hidden from view, as well as that which is visible. Wallach, for instance, asserts that landscape "begins with the values that comprise the substrate of all human geography and ends with all the visible manifestations of those values." To ignore the substructure behind any given landscape is to ignore the human forces that may be responsible for the creation of that landscape—forces associated with power, conflict, class, gender, and ethnicity. And of course landscape interpretation is also a highly subjective pursuit. As Cosgrove observes, "Landscape is not merely the world we see, it is a construction, a composition of that world." In the end, maintains Holdsworth, "All vision is subjective, and . . . all interpretation is personal."[4]

When it comes to subjectivity, much the same can be said of the various media—maps, paintings, lithographs, photographs—through which landscapes are represented and broadcast to a wider audience. Both J. B. Harley and Matthew Edney, for instance, have shown us how maps, those seemingly "passive reflections of the world of objects," have been constructed and employed to serve political ends. Through manipulation and falsification of content, through "silences" or omissions, and through promotion of ethnocentric views, maps down through the centuries have been used to concentrate and maintain power, preserve the status quo, and "desocialise" territory. Perhaps more obvious to the casual observer are the artistic liberties taken by landscape painters including those associated with the Hudson River school.[5]

Although our interest lies mainly with photographs, nineteenth-century lithographs—yet another form of landscape representation—merit brief mention and the reason is simple: before there were photographs, there were lithographs. According to planner and historian John W. Reps, Americans during the nineteenth century "seemed to have an insatiable yearning for pictures of all kinds. . . . Nothing failed to attract the interest of the public, escaped the eye of the artist, or lacked one or more lithographic publishers." This was particularly true where America's cities and towns were concerned. Between 1825 and 1875, thousands of lithographs of urban scenes were produced and sold in the United States. Placed on parlor walls or adorning the offices of local business-men, these marvelous bird's-eye, or "plan," views cast America's cities in the most flattering light, with freshly painted houses, prominent public buildings, clean streets, new railway lines, and smoking factories all proudly on display.[6]

While acknowledging the utility of lithographs as "visual slices of urban history" and as "selective records" of past human activity, geographer Richard Schein stresses that they cannot be interpreted as unbiased or innocent "reflections of a visual scene." Like other forms of landscape representation, lithographs were "material commodities that were authored, produced, marketed, sold, bought, displayed, and read." Schein notes for example that artists often presented sketches of their work to the public "to ensure that interested city residents' houses, offices, stores, and factories would be recognizable" in the final draft. Changes, such as the enlargement of a patron's building, could then be incorporated into the finished version. Thus Schein invites us to view landscapes and their representations (lithographs, photographs, maps) with a healthy modicum of suspicion so we may better position ourselves "to expose the secrets of their creation, order, ownership, control, and change."[7]

A Critical View of Photographs

In recent years, researchers from a broad spectrum of disciplines including American studies, anthropology, art history, geography, history, photography, and sociology have begun to view visual images—including photographs—with a more critical eye. As Mary Warner Marien, David Nye, Alan Trachtenberg, and numerous others have shown, photographs are more than mere visual images of past places and past activities. They are more than illustrative props or works of art. Archivist and geographer Joan Schwartz echoes these sentiments when she warns us that photographs are not "transcriptions of fact," but "social constructs capable of performing ideological work" that "vary in the way they are viewed and valued."[8]

Geographer Steven Hoelscher recently observed that photography has long benefited from a "reputation for scientific accuracy and unmediated truth." According to Hoelscher, our unswerving faith in photographs has much to do with the nature of photography itself:

> Photographs of geographical phenomena, when compared with other media, seem objective, true, and uncluttered by the whims of artists or the dictates of ideology. Born in the Victorian era from the seemingly perfect marriage of science and art, photography appeared to be the ideal medium for nature to copy herself with utter accuracy and exactitude; indeed, the notion that a photograph repeats its original . . . remains with us. The conventional idea of photography's infallibility is not a demonstrable truth, however, but a belief held with the irrational conviction of myth.

To this Schwartz adds that simply exhibiting the appearance of truth was enough to assure that the photograph was accepted as "a guarantee of objective and accurate representation." She continues: "From the widely held maxims that 'seeing is believing' and 'the camera does not lie,' it was a short leap of the imagination that allowed armchair travellers to believe they could acquire knowledge through the visual immediacy of photographs." This is not to say that photograph collections are not valuable repositories of information or that the scenes they depict are false. Far from it. Rather, it is a reminder that photographs are not neutral. Nor are they objective or innocent. Thus, writes historian and critic of photography Allan Sekula, we must "grasp the way in which photography constructs an imaginary world and passes it off as reality."[9]

Tuan notes that since classical times, Western tradition has accorded primacy to our sense of sight. While acknowledging the reasons for why this might be the case—chiefly, that richly detailed pictures are captivating, even seductive—Tuan wonders if we have truly considered the extent to which they can mislead us. In other words, are we fully aware of the biases and the limitations associated with the use of visual media? As the foregoing paragraphs suggest, the primacy we lend to visual media and the authority we extend to photographs in particular must be questioned. When working with photographs we would be wise to look beyond what is contained in the images themselves. We must, as Tuan admonishes us to do, view images with our mind's eye. To do so forces us to examine what is not visually apparent to us, for "images are mere pointers to an underlying reality that is not directly accessible to the eye." Therefore, we must ask: Who made the photographs? Who commissioned the photographs? Who published the photographs? Who participated in the creation of the "photographic document"? What purpose did the photographs serve? For whom were they intended? These are just a few of the questions that must be addressed if we are to move from simple and naive perception to a more sophisticated understanding.[10]

William Wyckoff and Lary M. Dilsaver's research on the Great Northern Railway photograph collection is a case in point. Focusing on the years 1911 to 1930, Wyckoff and Dilsaver investigated the role that photographs played in the company's "image-making campaign" to boost tourism at Glacier National Park. They conclude that the regional portraits manufactured by the Great Northern company were but selective and fragmentary representations of considerably more complex areas and, further, that low-cost, mass-produced photographs featured in company literature, popular magazines, and daily newspapers, were "carefully orchestrated reproductions of landscapes designed to communicate key elements of the Great Northern's visual iconography that was central to their Glacier Park marketing strategy." Exploring the context within which the Great Northern photographs were made, therefore, tells us much about how certain images are manufactured, packaged, and broadcast, and, more revealing, who stood to benefit from the distribution of a given version of "reality."[11]

Schwartz and Hoelscher have also reported on the link between photographs and travel in the nineteenth century. Like Wyckoff and Dilsaver, both authors emphasize the role that photographic images play in place making. According to Schwartz, the construction of place "resides not in the accuracy, but in the choice of individual views," which, taken together, yield "a carefully crafted portrayal of place." Hoelscher also maintains that photographic images are intimately involved in the creation of place. In much the same way that Tuan argued for a consideration of landscape as more than a collection of parts, Hoelscher avers: "Photography alone cannot mold nature. But it can direct our attention to things formerly overlooked—invisible and nonexistent—as it simultaneously organizes insignificant entities into significant composite wholes." Because humans control the place-making process—privileging certain images over others and including or excluding certain subjects—it is clear that the objectivity of any set of photographs must be brought into question and that multiple, perhaps competing, versions of reality are possible.[12]

Perhaps more so than any other publication of its kind, *National Geographic* is renowned the world over for its honest reporting and its objective and vivid photography. In their book *Reading* National Geographic, anthropologist Catherine A. Lutz and sociologist Jane L. Collins investigate the subtle and not so subtle ways in which the magazine's photographic images are constructed and manipulated prior to publication. While they note that individual photographers employed by the magazine often have "an independent and critical vision," the selection and editing process often serves to neutralize it. They conclude that *National Geographic*'s photographs send complex and often confusing messages. The *Geographic*'s tendency to shy away from controversial topics and images of human suffering, its policy of separating the production of photographs from caption writing, the scripting and posing associated with some shoots, and the practice of photographic sizing and enhancement (including computer alteration) were all identified as key elements that promoted the advancement of a particular view of the world. With respect to the latter, Lutz and Collins comment: "Officially, substantive alteration does not occur, but photographers, clearly critical, told stories about engravers who wanted to repair tears in the jackets of poverty-stricken Appalachian farmers or to add grass to barren landscapes. The speed and the ease with which such alterations can be made using new technologies vastly increases the temptation to do so," a point Fred Ritchin drives home convincingly.[13]

Several researchers have focused their attention on industrial scenes rather than travel photography. David Nye, for instance, has explored General Electric's use of photographs:

> The photographic department was a necessary part of this organization, taking much the same form in other corporations, such as General Motors, International Harvester, and the United States Rubber Company. Each required large numbers of images to improve internal communication and advertizing . . . to maintain a

strong market position, coordinate the vertical integration of their various enterprises, and deal with their work forces.

Jon M. Williams and Daniel T. Muir conclude that the purpose of DuPont's photographic endeavor shifted over time: "At first, photos were used for internal company information, but as the new technology for printing photographs developed, they were used increasingly for getting the DuPont Company message to the public." Originally used to convince stockholders that the business was viable, the DuPont images were later used to track the progress of construction projects, to record survey information, to keep the home office abreast of developments taking place at distant plants, to advertise and promote products, and to promote a sense of camaraderie among employees. Allan Sekula's work on the Dominion Steel and Coal Corporation archive confirms the value of photographs to the coal industry: "Large firms began to accumulate archives, and to employ photographers on a regular basis. Within the industrial firm, photographs were used to document capital improvements, to illustrate catalogues of industrial equipment, and ultimately to intervene directly in the labour process."[14]

Environmental historian Brian Black's recent work on the western Pennsylvania oil fields also warrants mention. Among the historical data sets Black uses to support his research is an impressive collection of photographs taken by John Mather. While they provide a stunning visual record of change in "Petrolia," closer inspection elevates their significance when we learn who the financial sponsors of the images were and why the images were taken in the first place. According to Black, "When wells came in, Mather was often called by owners to record the event in hopes of encouraging other investors. His lens could validate the well's success and chronicle its position in the history that was unfolding in the valley." Delving deeper, the scenes of devastation in western Pennsylvania's oil fields are, in Black's opinion, suggestive of

the free acceptance of massive change and the need to preserve a record of what would be lost by such change. . . . While at one level a photographic record such as Mather's preserves a chronicle of human technological supremacy over nature, it more specifically preserves a record of what is or will soon be lost through further technological advancement. In this way, photography is more the recording of activity upon a borderland, active with give and take from each side. . . . During the nineteenth century, industry and technology were so enmeshed in visions of economic, cultural, and social progress that almost any avenue for profit was acceptable.

Following this stream of thought, it becomes apparent that the landscapes we create say much about those who create them. The way we define, value, and ultimately treat natural resources, the manner in which we adopt and apply new technologies, and the ever-changing relationship between management and labor tells us much about our ethics, values, and priorities at any given point in time. So do the photographs we choose to make.[15]

Pennsylvania was not only a major producer of oil but of coal as well. Once its utility was firmly established, the relative abundance of this mineral and the ease with which it could be extracted ensured that it would figure prominently in the country's future energy plans for decades to come. Given the extraordinary growth of the industry during the late nineteenth and early twentieth centuries, the tremendous impact mining had on the physical environment, and the social and economic upheaval brought on by the Great Depression, it is not surprising that coal mining—much more so than oil drilling—attracted the attention of photographers. Indeed, as the following section shows, some of America's most talented photographers were drawn to Appalachia's coal-mining districts during the 1930s and 1940s.

The Farm Security Administration Project

Professor of American studies Robert Snyder remarks that the American South has had "a long, rich, variegated and influential photographic history." Some of the best-known and most influential photographs of the South were taken during the Great Depression, a time when photographers working for the federal government fanned out across the country to capture images of American life. One agency in particular, the Farm Security Administration (FSA), has been closely identified with this photographic effort. Historian Jerry Bruce Thomas writes:

> The most enduring national impact of the FSA came from its efforts to call attention to the plight of the rural poor through photographs, films, and books. These materials now form a rich source of information about the era's social and economic history. . . . The agency contracted with several outstanding photographers to record the conditions of rural life throughout the country. Some of

the photographs formed the basis for books such as Dorothea
Lange and Paul Taylor's *An American Exodus* (1939) and James
Agee and Walker Evans's *Let Us Now Praise Famous Men* (1941).

Many of the photographers employed by the Resettlement Administration (RA), Farm Security Administration, and Office of War Information—including Walker Evans, Russell Lee, Arthur Rothstein, Ben Shahn,
and Marion Post Wolcott—produced powerful images of everyday life
and labor in the isolated farming and mining communities of the mountain South.[16]

As time has passed, Evans, Shahn, Post, and Lange have become household names, at least in some quarters, and their black-and-white photographs are now celebrated for their artistic merit. Schwartz, for one, is
wary of any such shift in the treatment of photographs: "Elevated to art
icons, isolated from their contexts or consulted after the fact, photographs are robbed of their documentary power and cheated of their right-
ful place in geographical research and teaching." With respect to the FSA
collection, historian F. Jack Hurley acknowledges that we have developed
a "star system" approach to the study of these images: "We stand back,
view the beautiful print on the gallery wall and say, 'isn't it wonderful? It's
an Evans' (or Lange, or Lee, or whatever). This can lead to a dangerously
uncritical viewing of the work and even actual distortion of the nature of
the Farm Security project." As Hurley suggests, ignoring the historical
context within which the photographs were produced reduces the enormous assemblage of images to just that—an assemblage of images. The
significance of the photographs can only be understood if one explores
the federal government's motives for sponsoring the overall project, examines the ways in which the photographs were used, studies the tendencies
and practices of the individual photographers themselves, and acquires a
reasonable knowledge of the period when they were made. Even then, the
full weight of their influence and meaning may be lost.[17]

It should come as no surprise that key government administrators
were well aware of the power of photographs when it came to influencing
public opinion. Both Rexford Tugwell, head of the RA, and Roy Stryker,
chief of the Historical Unit (which was charged with the task of procur-
ing photographs), were, from the outset, willing to invoke the power of
this medium to garner support for President Franklin Delano Roosevelt's
many relief and recovery programs. Soon after the establishment of the
Resettlement Administration, the Historical Unit began to accumulate

pictures. According to Susan H. Edwards, "The RA/FSA photographic project evolved from a sophisticated awareness of a persuasive and propagandistic power of the medium—an agenda that manipulated perceived photographic truth for humanistic and political ends. . . . In addition to the government's plans to circulate images that illustrated the desperate need for government intervention, the photographs were available without cost for exhibition and publication." With regard to this last point, it should be noted that the photographs that were made were never intended for distribution among the subjects who were portrayed. And the photographers knew that their work would not be viewed by the majority of their subjects. This was not the purpose of the project. Rather, the photos were intended "to show the rest of the nation, and Washington especially, what life was like in Appalachia."[18]

Equally important is the fact that Stryker sent his photographers, save for Shahn, out into the field with detailed shooting scripts, identifying the regions they were to visit and the types of images the agency was interested in obtaining. This has led to charges that photographers staged shots to provide "propaganda for the U.S. government." However, it is unlikely that the federal government had any unseemly intentions when it assigned photographers to a particular area or requested that they return with images concentrated on a specific theme. Indications are that FSA photographers were concerned with the accuracy of their work and mindful of the limits of their medium. Nonetheless, it is also evident that they were devoted to the cause the government had taken up and imbued with a sense of urgency with regard to the plight of their human subjects.[19]

Another complicating factor comes into play when we take into account the habits, tendencies, political leanings—in a word, the individuality—of the photographer. A closer look at painter and photographer Ben Shahn is illustrative. In the fall of 1935, Shahn traveled by automobile through West Virginia and Kentucky and then pressed on into Arkansas, Mississippi, and Louisiana. The photographs he took attracted widespread attention to the impoverished conditions that had settled on the coal-mining communities and farms of the American South. According to Susan Edwards, Shahn's photographs were deeply influenced by his personal belief that the individuals he was capturing on film—the mountaineers, miners, tenant farmers, sharecroppers, and trappers of the South—were all victims of class stratification, racism, exploitative labor practices, and poverty. In analyzing one of his images, Edwards remarks,

In Shahn's 1935 photograph made in Freeze Fork, West Virginia, a lone miner walks along a railroad track at the crest of a mining community. Rows of identical company houses with outhouses line the dale below. A tree in the foreground is conspicuously isolated, punctuating the denuded, craggy landscape. The photograph's message, consistent with Shahn's personal convictions and grounded in his study of the writings of Saint-Simon and Karl Marx, is that the human cost of industrialization is the degradation and alienation of the individual. As capital is accumulated, the lot of the labourer worsens. Shahn was deeply moved by the harshness and hazards that coal miners endured day to day.

Shahn's photographs must, therefore, be understood as critiques of the prevailing economic system and not mere portraits of poverty and despair. While the images drew much-needed attention to the region, Edwards argues that the "coded messages" of the photographs "not only propagated the government's agenda, but also perpetuated regional and racial stereotypes."[20]

The "objectivity" and "truthfulness" of photographs is again cast into doubt when we compare the work of Marion Post Wolcott and Doris Ulmann. According to Melissa McEuen, "Although both photographers expressed similar reactions to the region and to its people, and travelled much of the same ground in eastern Kentucky, their respective photographic studies yielded strikingly different results." Ulmann, who planned and financed her trips and was not an employee of the federal government, elected to emphasize in her work the rugged individualism and personal talents of her subjects. Convinced that the "rich diversity of regional cultures" she came across was threatened by industrialization and modernization, Ulmann wanted to compile a record of their existence. Post, who was hired by the FSA after Walker Evans and Dorothea Lange departed, chose to focus her attention on "particular social lives and social connections." McEuen implies that the dramatic differences that distinguish Ulmann's image of Appalachia from Post's view "can be traced to the messages each woman wanted to deliver."[21]

The evidence I have presented thus far has shown that photographs are not the objective and neutral records we have sometimes made them out to be. They are not "transcriptions of facts." Nor do they represent "unmediated truth." As Nye comments, "Photographs do not mirror reality; they are social constructions. They are made." In the hands of different makers, they are infused with different messages. In the hands of different social and cultural institutions, they are assigned different tasks. In the hands of different viewers, they take on different meanings. Hence the need to handle them with care and ask, as geographer Mona Domosh would have us do, some pointed and probing questions:

> Visual material—photographs, advertisements, and newspaper images—are discursive forms, and need to be interpreted as documents of culture, or as "texts." These images are not transparent conveyors of "truth," but instead participate in the creation of meaning. Yet many historical geographers use images either as background material or as historical documents of past truths, seemingly unaware of the politics of representation. What is being obscured when we ignore the discursive production and interpretation of visual material? What are appropriate methods for conducting that interpretation?[22]

To this point, I have tried to draw attention to the power and attraction of photographs. Clearly, photographs are a unique archival source that can enhance our ability to reconstruct the past. As Black points out, the rise of professional photography made it possible "to freeze a nonrepeatable event" and make it "available for future consideration." In this way, historical photographs permit us to establish at least some semblance of a baseline against which we can measure and assess change. If read carefully, photographs can also tell us much about the society or environment in which they were produced, as well as the priorities and values of their makers.[23]

On the other hand, photographs have their limitations. The very act of producing a photograph invokes a kind of power that privileges the photographer over the photographed. Because we can never see all that there is to see—or all that the photographer sees—we must concern ourselves with that which is not shown—an exercise that calls into question the "unmediated truth" of the photograph and the objectivity of the photographer. At best, photographs can provide us with only an illusion (albeit a powerful one) of having experienced a place or an event. With respect to travel photography, for example, Schwartz comments: "Gone . . . were the sounds of foreign languages and strange music, the taste of exotic foods, the smells of wafting fragrances and awful stench, and the feel of searing heat and bitter cold. To know a place was to know what it *looked like*—in black and white. Ultimately, the photographic excursion

Fig. 1.1. "No. 212 opening 1916."

denied the armchair traveller an integrated sensory experience." In the end, according to Holdsworth, "Visual information . . . can be a useful catalyst for both research and, especially, teaching. But it can rarely stand alone in providing convincing explanations about questions of human geography." Thus the need to investigate the forces that lay hidden behind all cultural landscapes—the forces that shape the landscapes we view in the photographic record, as well as the forces that shape the photographic record itself.[24]

The Consolidation Coal Company Photograph Collection

As intimated in the introduction, the federal government was not the only entity documenting life and labor in the mining communities of central and southern Appalachia at this time. Coal companies were also collecting and commissioning images from the Southern mountains. An especially rich archive, the Consolidation Coal Company collection contains nearly four thousand photographs and is housed in the Agriculture

Fig. 1.2. "No. 201 tipple, July 10, 1913."

and Natural Resources Collection at the National Museum of American History in Washington, D.C. Images of mine openings and tailings, mining equipment and machine shops, tipples, mining accidents and safety demonstrations, as well as scenes from the company towns—worker housing, schools, churches, hospitals, gardens, recreational facilities, holiday celebrations, and company store displays, to name but a few (figs. 1.1–4). Focusing on the company's principle properties in Kentucky and West Virginia, but also including activities in several other states such as Maryland, Pennsylvania, Virginia, Ohio, and Wisconsin, the photographs provide powerful insights into what life was like in Consolidation's coal mines and coal towns during the first half of the twentieth century, at least as seen through the eyes of company photographers.[25]

In 1960, Charles O. Houston Jr., associate curator in the Division of Manufactures and Heavy Industries for the Smithsonian Institution's National Museum of History and Technology, contacted the Beth-Elkhorn Corporation, owners of the Consolidation Coal Company photograph

Fig. 1.3. "School and Pupils at Mine No. 37 12-9-18."

collection. Houston was interested in acquiring the collection and show-ing some of the images in the museum's Hall of Coal exhibit. Two years later, Houston and Dr. P. W. Bishop, head curator in the Department of Arts and Manufactures, acquired the collection from the Beth-Elkhorn Corporation (Bethlehem Mines Corporation) in Jenkins, Kentucky. Soon after the acquisition, the photographs and the official papers describing the collection were misplaced in storage at the museum. However, the photographs were recovered in 1987 after a reorganization of the agricul-ture and natural resources storage room. Museum specialists have since catalogued the photographs and provided researchers and other parties with improved access to the collection.[26]

While the total number of photographs approaches four thousand, it is clear that the original collection was larger. Based on the documentary evidence that has survived, it is difficult to say how many images were taken originally or what fraction of the total is represented. While the

Fig. 1.4. "4th July Celebration Jenkins, Ky. 7-4-27."

identities of individual photographers are not presently known, stamps on the back of approximately five hundred of the prints indicate they were produced by the J. E. Brown studio of Stamford, Connecticut. Although many of the photographs were unmounted at the time of acquisition in 1962, it is likely that most had been included in company albums at one time—probably assembled for display at company offices.[27]

What compelled Consolidation Coal to maintain a photographic record of their activities? The overarching goal was to project—in a sense to advertise—a positive image of Consolidation's operations to potential investors. This appears to have been the primary purpose of the company albums. As ensuing chapters will show, however, different photographs in the collection were taken to satisfy different needs. Some photos were woven into company histories and other promotional materials. Others were used for training or insurance purposes. Still others made their way into the pages of the company's *Mutual Monthly Magazine,* which was published monthly, and later, bimonthly, between approximately 1918 and 1928. Of course, the editors of this company journal were interested in more than the dissemination of company-related news. They had a much more ambitious goal. By openly espousing the principles of "Americanism" and stressing the importance of law and order, as well as obedience to employer and loyalty to country, Consolidation's Employment Relationship Department was engaged in a conscious effort to influence the behavior and productivity of the company's workforce.[28]

While there are numerous ways to analyze the photographs in the Smithsonian collection, a particularly manageable approach is to divide them into three broad categories: the company town, work and equipment, and images associated with environmental alteration. Careful review of the entire collection, however, reveals several underlying themes that may not be obvious to the casual observer perusing a select few photos. These themes include strategies related to corporate paternalism, evidence of racial segregation as well as of social and cultural diversity, and the impact of industrial capitalism on the landscape.

A word of caution is in order before proceeding further. Whether it is the steep slopes, the solid trains of coal cars loaded high with varied grades of black diamonds, the arrangement of buildings in a company town, or some other such sign, it is readily apparent that the viewer of this collection is dealing with an Appalachian scene. Stereotypically Appalachian features have been transmitted to us in many and varied ways over the years via television news programs and documentaries, newspapers and magazines, Hollywood films, and works of fiction. The result is that much of what has been produced has presented a distorted view of this enormous region, inspiring some to cast away the exaggerated and sensational portraits of Appalachia in favor of finding the "real" Appalachia. As geographer Stephen P. Hanna has argued persuasively, however, "there is no real Appalachian space that precedes or exists outside of its representation. All images contribute to Appalachia as known and experienced and, therefore, cannot be judged for accuracy through comparison to a real region." It is not, therefore, my intention to follow in the footsteps of individuals preoccupied with the search for the "real" Appalachia. Nor am I especially interested in uncovering the "truth" about the Consolidation Coal Company. Rather, it is my wish to place the photographs in this collection in historical context and to examine the variety of ways they might be interpreted. In the process, we will no doubt become familiar with the many faces of Appalachia they represent. The first step in this process necessarily involves taking a closer look at the Consolidation Coal Company—a topic to which we turn in the next chapter.[29]

A Time for Consolidation, 1860–1945

Why should we voyage to far foreign shore
The beauties of nature to see
When in Maryland's hills they are found by the score
As perfect as nature can be.

—"Old Allegany," 1919

I Starting Point

In his 1983 book *Theirs Be the Power: The Moguls of Eastern Kentucky* lawyer Harry M. Caudill examines the complex web of political and social relationships that ultimately "transformed a remote and impoverished hinterland into the nation's most productive coal field." Its pages recount the exploits of predatory speculators, avaricious robber barons, and ruthless politicians who, working in concert, imposed a harsh new set of realities on the Cumberland Plateau. While the coal that was removed contributed greatly to America's rise to industrial prominence, in time the negative effects of absentee ownership, corporate control, and mineral extraction took their toll on local economies and the physical environment. To understand the industrial transformation that took place in eastern Kentucky and across the Appalachian South, however, Caudill instructs us to direct our attention elsewhere: "The juggernaut that would overwhelm Kentucky was born in Maryland. The Appalachian mineral fields have been called an economic colony owned and governed for the profit of eastern banks, corporations, and tax-exempt foundations. The capture of Appalachia and the rendering out of its wealth for the benefit of absentee owners began in the coal-rich hills and valleys of Maryland's Allegany County." By tracing the roots of eastern Kentucky's industrial transformation to western Maryland, Caudill clearly recognized that this place was one of the first in the country to experience the effects of large-scale coal-mining operations. Not inconsequentially, it was also one of the first to be affected by the transportation revolution initiated by railroads and canals. As historian Crandall A. Shifflett has pointed out, "All of the land and coal was worthless . . . if it could not be gotten out of its mountain redoubts. There was no use to open mines if the coal could not be transported to distant markets."[1]

By 1842 the nation's first commercial railroad, the Baltimore and Ohio (B&O), had reached Cumberland, Maryland, effectively linking the "coal-rich hills and valleys" of the western part of the state with the bustling urban centers of the Atlantic seaboard. Eight years later, the Chesapeake and Ohio Canal (C&O) reached its western terminus, connecting Cumberland with Georgetown, on the lower Potomac River. With the railroad and canal in place, exploitation of mineral resources—the rights to which had been acquired, in some cases, decades earlier—could be carried out on a scale that previously had not been possible. As was the case in Maryland, Pennsylvania, West Virginia, and elsewhere the railroad played a critical role in linking these remote areas to key markets.[2]

Perhaps more important, however, western Maryland was the birthplace of the Consolidation Coal Company—a business venture that would eventually develop into the largest bituminous coal company in the United States. Indeed, it was here in western Maryland, one could argue, that a pattern of land acquisition, absentee ownership, and corporate control was established that would spread to West Virginia, western Pennsylvania, and eastern Kentucky as the railroad pushed further and further into the mountains. And so it is here, in the Georges Creek valley, that our story begins.

Corporate Antecedents

In the far western portion of Allegany County, just west of the Appalachian front, Georges Creek wends its way from near the Maryland-Pennsylvania border through a narrow valley and enters the north branch of the Potomac River at Westernport. The most striking geologic feature of the valley—one that early explorers, including George Washington, noticed early on—was the existence of vast deposits of semibituminous coal. Approximately twenty-seven coal beds were identified by 1845, resulting in an aggregate thickness of seventy-six and two-thirds feet. Renowned British geologist Charles Lyell, who visited the area in the 1840s, likened the shape of the successive beds of coal to "a great number of canoes placed one within another." One of these beds, the Pittsburgh seam, or Big Vein as it came to be known, measured approximately fourteen to sixteen feet in thickness. On the subject of the quality of what would come to be called Georges Creek coal, historian J. Thomas Scharf in 1882 wrote that it was widely celebrated for its "freedom from impurities of all kinds, especially sulphur."[3]

Beginning in the first decade of the nineteenth century, small quantities were sent down the Potomac River via flatboat to Georgetown, along with lumber and some agricultural goods. Transport of this sort was possible only during the spring season, when waters on the river were high. Upon arrival, the boats were dismantled and their crews walked home. Although limited, by 1820 the Maryland coal trade was becoming commercially important. From the perspective of the early years of the nineteenth century, coal's future looked bright and all indications were that it could only get brighter. As one promoter put it frankly in 1855, "The vast industrial and social importance of a *cheap* and *abundant* supply of mineral fuel, is daily becoming more generally realized, and the inquiry into the precise conditions which regulate this supply, is one which more or less occupies the mind of every intelligent person."[4]

Given the increase in demand for coal spurred on by industrialization, the existence of coal so near to the Atlantic seaboard aroused interest among local boosters and East Coast businessmen wishing to purchase mineral lands and mine them for profit. Before taking such a risk, prospective investors employed geologists, civil engineers, and other experts as surveyors to evaluate the coalfield for its potential. The reports were extremely favorable. An 1836 report from geologist John Powell to the Boston and New York Coal Company, for instance, declared that the quality of Georges Creek coal rivaled that of the finest European coals. In another assessment, David Mushet commented: "The specimen of coal sent is the very best bituminous coal I have ever met with." Yale professor of chemistry, metallurgy, and geology Benjamin Silliman examined much of the Georges Creek valley in 1838 and 1839 for prospective mining interests. In concluding one of these reports, Silliman remarked:

> In geological structure—in natural facilities for drainage and
> extraction—in the excellence and peculiar character of the coal—
> in its vast abundance—in its relations to the iron—the limestone—
> the fire clays—the sand stones for building the forests—the agricul-
> ture and pasturage—the climate—the position in reference to the
> Western waters and the Atlantic—the national road, and the
> Chesapeake and Ohio Canal,—and in a word, the entire group of
> its advantages, it is not excelled by any coal field in our country,
> while it is equalled by few, if any, in the world.

One aspect of the Yale professor's account that is especially revealing are his comments regarding the quantity of coal to be found in the Georges Creek valley. In 1838 he noted that the coal "is so abundant that it will not be exhausted for centuries." In 1839 he stated that "the body of coal is so large and continuous as wholly to dispel any idea of its being exhausted." This belief that resources, both mineral and timber, existed in "inexhaustible" quantities is a recurrent one in the coal development literature.[5]

Another appraisal was obtained from George W. Hughes, a U.S. civil engineer. In 1837 Hughes's glowing account included the following statement:

> It seems as if nature, in a freak of prodigality, had bestowed, with
> a lavish hand, her choicest blessings in the county of Alleghany
> [sic]. She has given her a magnificent river for a boundary; a climate
> mild, equable, and healthy; a soil rich in fruits and agricultural pro-
> ductions; luxuriant ranges for vast herds of cattle; water whole-
> some and abundant, and mineral treasures almost immeasurable in
> extent and incalculable in value.

Another examination, this one carried out by Henry Thomas Weld, confirmed the findings of Silliman and Hughes. As the following passage suggests, his report also revealed an attitude that was quite common at the time—namely that the natural world existed for human purposes: "But Nature, seemingly unwilling that so large a portion of her work should remain comparatively useless to mankind, herself provided a means which in the lapse of ages would unfold to man the secrets of the Alleghany coalfield, at the same time affording him facilities for using the knowledge so obtained to the best advantage." Experts generally agreed that the coal measures compared favorably to those located in Scotland, England, and Wales and that the prospects for successful mining operations were very good.[6]

Favorable reports regarding the development prospects of the region enticed Eastern businessmen, in particular, into action. During the first half of the nineteenth century, corporations interested in mining coal and iron ore and cutting timber, and backed by capital from centers of commerce such as New York, Baltimore, Boston, and London, began accumulating property rights in the area, a process that was mediated by speculators, some of whom were also local residents. Between approximately 1828 and 1850, a total of thirty coal or coal-and-iron companies were incorporated by Maryland's general assembly. While not all these ventures proved successful, the future pattern of landownership had, nevertheless, been set. On the eve of the arrival of the Baltimore and Ohio Railroad to Cumberland in 1842, much of the Maryland coal region was controlled not by yeoman farmers and squatters but by a procession of speculators and corporate interests.[7]

The first commercial coal venture to locate in the valley was the Maryland Mining Company. Incorporated by the Maryland legislature on 12 March 1829, its owners were authorized to acquire five thousand acres of land and construct a railroad from their mines to Cumberland. According to one source, the president and the directors were also "authorized to open a banking business, to be located in Cumberland and called the Mineral Bank, with the proviso that the bank should have no connection with the railroad. Just what the legislators of that day meant by 'no connection,' when the directorates of the mining company and the bank were to be identical, is rather hard to determine today!" Nearly eight years would pass, however, before the Maryland Mining Company acquired property. Charles E. Beachley, whose 1934 *History of the Consolidation Coal Company* was published on the seventieth anniversary of that company's first shipment of coal, offered the following explanation for the delay: "Perhaps their lack of action is explained by the circumstances that no less than five charters to different mining and railroad companies were granted at the same session. If every proposed mine had been opened, and every projected railroad built, the combined capacity would have been ten times greater than any possible demand for coal for years to come." Although first to incorporate, the Maryland Mining Company never achieved financial success. By 1851, the year company president Matthew

St. Clair Clarke died, financial ruin was on the horizon. That Clarke was delinquent on state and county taxes may have been a harbinger of things to come. In September 1852 the company's holdings—including the railroad connecting Eckhart Mines to Wills Creek, nineteen hundred acres of land, and the town of Eckhart Mines—were acquired by the Cumberland Coal and Iron Company at public sale. Although not a financial success, the significance of the Maryland Mining Company lived on, however, as it was the earliest corporate antecedent of the powerful Consolidation Coal Company.[8]

How can we explain the financial difficulties experienced by companies like the Maryland Mining Company, especially in light of the enthusiastic reports submitted by engineers and geologists like those mentioned earlier? A review of the problems that beset another mining concern, the Maryland and New York Iron and Coal Company, will perhaps provide some answers. In 1838 a group led by Lewis Howell and backed by English capital obtained a charter from the Maryland legislature incorporating the Maryland and New York Iron and Coal Company and giving its owners permission to construct a railroad from its mines in Allegany County to the Chesapeake and Ohio Canal at or near Cumberland. Unfortunately for the company, the road was not completed until 1845. In addition, completion of the canal—upon which many companies based their calculations—was delayed until 1850 due to construction and labor problems. A more disturbing development centered around the accuracy of the aforementioned geological surveys. According to Beachley, the Maryland and New York Iron and Coal Company was "handicapped by inadequate knowledge." More specifically he writes, "At that date, the extent of the coal deposits was unknown. Popular belief ascribed rich coal deposits to all the hills in Allegany County. The lands the company purchased, often at fabulous prices, had little coal under them, which must have been a grievous disappointment when work was fairly begun."[9]

With respect to the name of the company, it should be noted that iron ore deposits figured prominently in the minds and plans of early speculators and investors in Allegany County. This was certainly the case with the Maryland and New York Iron and Coal Company. At Mount Savage in 1840, Howell's company established an iron works that four years later would roll the first iron rails manufactured in the United States. Despite this historic achievement, the venture failed—the Allegany County iron deposits were not sufficient to make the business profitable. In 1847 the *Cumberland Alleganian* reported:

These works were sold by the Sheriff of Allegany county, on Thursday last, to satisfy judgments against the company in favor of Cary & Forbes, of New York, and Messrs. Wright, Palmer & Weld, trustees for the English bond holders. We understand that the sale was made at $215,000—and that the purchasers are Messrs. Corning & Winslow, of Albany, N.Y. and Mr. J. M. Forbes, of Boston. The purchasers are said to be gentlemen of capital, practically acquainted with the iron business, which encourages the hope that at an early day Mt. Savage will again be the theatre of an active business. We also learn that the purchasers will blend their interests in the "Lulworth Iron Company."

In addition to the rolling mill, furnaces, nine-mile railroad, and brick-yard, approximately forty-eight hundred acres were conveyed. The Lulworth Iron Company later amended its charter and became the Mount Savage Iron Company in 1848. As the preceding newspaper passage suggests, some of America's preeminent merchants took an active interest in Maryland's nascent iron industry. Among them was John Murray Forbes. Indeed, it was Forbes's intention to make the Mount Savage Iron Works "the great Iron Co. of this Country." By the 1850s, however, even Forbes had had enough of the iron business. In a letter to his cousin Paul in 1859, he wrote, "Its [*sic*] a big business & ought not to be lightly touched by Amateurs like you & me."[10]

A Time for Consolidation

The years 1861 to 1865 had a tremendous effect on the development of the coal industry in western Maryland and elsewhere. In their classic history of the United States, Allan Nevins and Henry Steele Commager note that the Civil War "gave an immense stimulus to industry, speeded up the exploitation of natural resources, the development of large-scale manufacturing, the rise of investment banking, the extension of foreign commerce, and brought to the fore a new generation of 'captains of industry' and 'masters of capital.'" To borrow from Nevins and Commager again, "No other generation in American history witnessed changes as swift or as revolutionary as those which transformed the rural republic of Lincoln and Lee into the urban industrial empire of Roosevelt and Rockefeller." Historian Duane Smith is even more succinct: "In the post–Civil War years, business and industry became enthroned in the temple of success."[11]

In the Georges Creek valley, it was during this period in particular that we see smaller companies combine to form larger and more powerful conglomerates. As George H. Love, president of the Pittsburgh Consolidation Coal Company, explained on the occasion of his 1955 address to the Newcomen Society of America, "an overwhelming urge to consolidate" mining efforts in the valley took place at this time "not to get larger but as an attempt to meet the drastic competition always present in a natural resource industry with excess capacity." Regardless of the motive behind the effort to consolidate—and Love's assertion is certainly open to debate—the growth of combinations had the effect of increasing absentee ownership and concentrating power and wealth in the hands of a relatively small group of businessmen.[12]

The fact that many of these large companies were headquartered outside the region was a source of consternation for many living in the valley. In 1865 one contributor to the editorial page of the *Cumberland Union and Allegany County Gazette* opined:

If our monied corporations could see anything more than money—if they could realize that men are not "dumb driven cattle," and no man or company of men can ever so regard and treat them without cursing them and being cursed themselves, then there would be some comfort in seeing great corporations form around us . . . their general effect is to degrade and un-man us. They put much money into the hands of a few at the expense of the many; and once the few have got the money they care not one straw for the many who were fools enough to contribute it.

Such "freely expressed community hostility toward New York capitalists" eventually prompted several companies to move their headquarters to Cumberland or, short of that, Baltimore by the 1880s.[13]

Like it or not, great corporations were forming in the Georges Creek valley and beyond in western Maryland. By far the largest and most powerful conglomerate to emerge in the valley was the Consolidation Coal Company. Created from the combined interests of several companies, Consolidation Coal was granted a charter by the Maryland legislature in March 1860 but did not begin shipping coal east from the Georges Creek valley until four years later. In May 1864 its capital stock was increased from one hundred thousand to six million dollars,

whereupon it acquired the following properties in exchange for stock: Ocean Steam Coal Company: lands and real estate in

Allegany County, Maryland, approximately 2,345 ⅛ acres, in exchange for 16,000 shares of capital stock. Frostburg Coal Company: lands, tenements, and property in Allegany County, Maryland, approximating 1,687 ¼ acres, together with land, wharf, and river front at Alexandria, Virginia, and all other railroad property wheresoever situate, with rolling stock, etc., in exchange for 12,000 shares of capital stock. Mount Savage Iron Company: lands and tenements in Allegany County, Maryland, approximating 6,890 acres, together with machinery, tools, and other personal property of every description wheresoever situate, including the Cumberland and Pennsylvania Railroad, its equipment, etc., in exchange for 22,000 shares of capital stock.

According to Beachley, "The acquisition of these properties is generally credited to William H. Aspinwall of New York who, with his associates, had previously purchased a tract extending across the Georges Creek basin in the neighborhood of Squirrel Neck and Wright's Run, and had organized the Ocean Steam Coal Company."[14]

On 31 May 1869, a further attempt at consolidation of coal interests was unveiled, coming in the form of an open letter to coal operators in western Maryland:

To the Stockholders of the Companies Mining Cumberland COAL in Allegany County, Maryland:

An experience of 25 years has convinced many of the most practical and sagacious persons, whose interests have been identified with the development of the Cumberland Coal Mines, that those interests can only be made reasonably remunerative by a complete change in the system of management. The total product of 1,708 tons in 1842 has been increased by the legitimate demands of the trade, to 1,330,443 tons in 1868, with a prospect of 1,500,000 tons in 1869, and yet, of the immense capital which has been invested in Allegany County, in coal property, how large a proportion has been swept away, and of that now representing the mining interests how insignificant is the proportion which, even occasionally, makes any return to the proprietors. Three reasons may be given to explain these unsatisfactory results. First, remoteness from our principal markets, with insufficiency and high cost of transportation hereto; second, heavy expenses of multiplied administration, and third, ruinous and under existing circumstances, uncontrollable competition.

The first of these obstacles would inevitably subside, if not disappear under a systematic and unified apportionment of production to demand; the second and third would obviously vanish by the substitution of a single management, in the common interest, for the twenty-one separate organizations which, with their complicated and expensive machinery, now absorb the modicum of profit which is left to the owners of the mines.

Five of the largest companies having, with others, tried for years, but in vain, to remedy the evils above averted to, by harmony of action, have at length determined to find, if practicable, a solution of the problem by uniting their properties under one organization, permanent and homogeneous. A suitable agent has been selected to investigate the relative areas and values of their respective coal lands, preliminary, it is hoped, to the adoption of an equitable basis of incorporation. These five companies are now moving in perfect accord toward that object, and have established a joint committee on consolidation. Within a month it is hoped that they will be prepared to proceed to the consideration of such a basis. To this end it is earnestly desired that as many companies now operating in the Cumberland coal region of Allegany County should unite in having their lands surveyed and appraised; or, if not that, that they will, at least, appoint a representative, or more than one but not more than three, to meet with the joint committee and discuss with them the bearings of this scheme on their various interests. Stockholders are earnestly requested to press this important subject upon the consideration of their directors.

Communications may be addressed to either of the officers of the joint committee whose names are affixed, representing the American, Borden, Consolidation, Cumberland Coal and Iron and Hampshire and Baltimore companies.

> Allan Campbell, President
> Cumberland Coal and Iron Co.,
> Chairman, Joint Committee,
> 90 Broadway
> James S. Mackie, Vice President,
> The Consolidation Coal Company,

Secretary, Joint Committee,
71 Broadway

A newspaper report dated 26 January 1870 stated that "negotiations are now pending" with the Cumberland Coal and Iron Company, the Borden Mining Company, the American Coal Company, and the Hampshire and Baltimore Coal Company.[15]

In some quarters at least, reaction to the further consolidation of coal companies was anything but positive. In an editorial written to the *Cumberland Alleganian,* a resident of Georges Creek wrote,

> I understand that there is a project now on foot to consolidate the Cumberland Coal and Iron Company, its wharf and its railroad, with the Consolidation Coal Company, its wharf and its railroad. . . . Thus we are to have an overwhelming corporation, owning *all* the railroads and all the rolling stock used in the development of our coal region. Let me ask what is the object these non-residents of the State are striking at in getting up these consolidations? The object is patent to every reflective mind. It is to strike down all competition of the smaller companies in the coal region; to grasp all the railroads used for transporting coal and thus to control the coal interests. . . . Now, sir, is it prudent in the people of Maryland to stand silently by until this destruction of our best interests is accomplished by a scheming set of New York and Boston speculators?

Another article suggested that miners and others were also lined up against further consolidation:

> In the House of Delegates, on Saturday last, Mr. Kean presented a memorial of 350 citizens of Allegany county, interested in the coal trade as miners and otherwise, for an amendment to the charter of the Consolidation Coal Company of Allegany county—The paper states that the act of 1860, chap. 265, incorporating the "Consolidation Coal Company," is in direct defiance of the letter and spirit of the declaration of rights, which declares that "monopolies are odious, & c., and ought not be suffered." . . . The petitioners further show that a consolidation of nearly all the coal companies of Allegany county is about being effected under the unlimited power and authority given by said act of incorporation,

and thus a vast monopoly is now being established, dangerous to the liberty and independence of the people, and which will prevent all fair competition by other companies.

A union of these four enterprises with Consolidation Coal did not occur, however. For all the "high hopes of the signatory companies" and several months of work, the "suitable agent"—mining geologist J. T. Hodges—submitted a report deemed unsatisfactory by a number of the interested parties, ending the "perfect accord" mentioned in the circular. One of the interested parties, the American Coal Company, was lauded in the press for its refusal to accept the plan. Others, however, were willing to join forces with Consolidation Coal. In 1870, Consolidation added to its already extensive holdings when it absorbed the Cumberland Coal and Iron Company, the second largest coal company in the region and the one, it will be recalled, that had acquired the Maryland Mining Company eighteen years earlier. In addition to seven thousand acres of coal lands, Consolidation Coal acquired the Eckhart Branch Railroad; the Astor, Eckhart, and Hoffman mines; canal boats; wharves at Cumberland and Baltimore; New York barges; and other real estate. In less than a decade, expansion had allowed Consolidation to advance from sixth place to first in the shipping of Maryland's renowned bituminous coal.[16]

Subsequent purchases over the course of the next year gave Consolidation Coal control over five-sixths of the Big Vein coal in the region. By this time, Consolidation also possessed three outlets for the coal: one to the B&O Railroad at Cumberland; one to the B&O at Piedmont, West Virginia, across the Potomac River from Westernport, Maryland; and one to the C&O Canal at Cumberland via the Eckhart Branch or the Cumberland and Pennsylvania Railroad. Yet another connection, this one with the Pennsylvania Railroad, was established in 1871. In addition, Consolidation had its own wharves at Cumberland, Georgetown, Alexandria, and Baltimore and its own schooners to transport its products to seaboard cities. In this way did the Consolidation Coal Company come to dominate the coal trade of Allegany County.[17]

By 1871, Consolidation's board of directors consisted of ten individuals, all of whom resided in New York or Boston. Included on the board at this time were such corporate luminaries as Warren Delano, John Murray Forbes, James Roosevelt, and William Aspinwall. Harry Caudill writes that James Roosevelt's directorships "sound like a roll call of the major enterprises that were forging industrial America in the last half of the nineteenth century: railroads, steamboats, canals (including one in Nicaragua), banks, trust companies, coal, and the first holding company of its kind." Beginning in 1851, Roosevelt also worked briefly in the New York law firm of Benjamin Douglas Silliman, nephew of the Yale professor mentioned earlier in this chapter. Not coincidentally, one of the most important clients of the law firm was the Consolidation Coal Company of Maryland.[18]

Opposition or no opposition, the days of consolidation of business interests in western Allegany County were far from over. During the mid-1870s, the B&O Railroad, out of competition with the Pennsylvania Railroad, acquired large blocks of Consolidation Coal Company stock. In 1876, Robert Garrett, then the third vice president of the B&O, was added to the board of directors. In addition, a number of B&O directors were made directors of Consolidation. According to Beachley, "Thus Baltimore financiers secured control of the largest bituminous coal producing company in the country, and the Baltimore and Ohio Railroad was automatically assured the large revenues from the coal trade of Allegany County." And so through stock ownership and interlocking directorships in Consolidation Coal, the B&O sought to establish a monopoly over the Maryland coal industry.[19]

Local reaction to the B&O's takeover of Consolidation Coal was generally unfavorable. The *Cumberland Alleganian and Daily Times* for 11 November 1876 concluded that the results of the B&O's actions would be detrimental to the region: "The effect of the Baltimore road gaining control of the Consolidation company will, we believe, be injurious to the coal interest of Allegany county, for it will then be the only outlet for our production." Over the next few decades, the interests of both Consolidation Coal and the B&O became inextricably intertwined. This was most clearly reflected by the individuals who held positions of great responsibility and power in both organizations. Charles Mayer, for instance, who was elected president of Consolidation Coal in 1877, became president of the B&O in 1888. Mayer was well qualified for his new office, having served as president of the Despard Coal Company in West Virginia, director of the Western National Bank, and head of the firm Mayer, Carroll and Company. As Consolidation's top executive, writes Scharf, Mayer was president "of this great Maryland property, second only in importance in the State to the Baltimore and Ohio Railroad." Leonor F. Loree was another example, having served as president of the B&O in 1901, about which time the Pennsylvania Railroad began acquiring large holdings in the B&O, and then as a Consolidation Coal Company director from 1902 to 1904.[20]

The relationship did not continue indefinitely, however. During April 1906 the B&O sold its entire holdings of Consolidation stock to a Baltimore syndicate. To quote Beachley, "Thus did the railroad relinquish control of large mining operations in the best known soft coal regions of the country and of extensive distributing companies in the leading markets of both the east and the west." The sale was prompted by an Interstate Commerce Commission investigation into the relations between coal companies and coal-carrying railroads.[21]

By 1880 the Consolidation Coal Company controlled fifteen thousand acres of land "whose surface is either covered with valuable timber or fertile farms, all of which is underlaid with workable veins of coal. More than 7,000 acres of it hold the famous 'Big Vein,' yielding 10,000 tons to the acre, and lying nearer to market than the lands of any other company in the region." Over the next twenty or so years, Consolidation Coal confined its operations to western Maryland. Output of coal continued to increase and the company continued to prosper thanks in large part to the support of influential Eastern investors.[22]

Expansion

Meanwhile, during the latter years of the nineteenth century, newspapers directed an increasing amount of attention toward the natural resources of Pennsylvania and West Virginia and the activities of such politician-developers as Henry G. Davis, Stephen B. Elkins, Johnson N. Camden, and Clarence W. Watson. By 1852 the B&O had "blasted its way over the Allegheny Mountains," providing service to Fairmont and beyond, and thus opening up the coalfields of northern West Virginia. The following year, the Pennsylvania Railroad crossed the mountains to Pittsburgh, initiating development of the valuable coal fields in Cambria and Somerset Counties. An article focused on the "undeveloped riches" of West Virginia in the 11 June 1903 edition of the *Cumberland Alleganian* is suggestive of the booster spirit of the day, as well as the extent to which parts of the state remained "untapped," even at the beginning of the twentieth century. It is also reminiscent of what one might have read about the Georges Creek valley several decades earlier:

The undeveloped riches of West Virginia are beyond all knowledge. The state possesses all the advantages which have made Western Pennsylvania one of the most opulent portions of the United States. The coal deposits of West Virginia are of enormous extent and almost inexhaustible in quantity. It has petroleum and natural gas, iron and other minerals, clay, sand and every variety of stone. It has great areas of forest where the sound of the woodman's ax has never been heard and besides these things fertile fields and extensive pasture lands.[23]

In time the "drift towards combination" spread elsewhere. In western Pennsylvania several small operators combined to form the Monongahela River Consolidated Coal and Coke Company, which would later become part of the Pittsburgh Coal Company. In central Pennvania the same "urge" built the Somerset Coal Company. Similar movements were occurring elsewhere toward the end of the nineteenth century, most notably in northern West Virginia, where several mining concerns combined to form the Fairmont Coal Company and Clarksburg Fuel Company, and in eastern Kentucky, where men like Richard M. Broas and John C. C. Mayo were accumulating hundreds of thousands of acres of mineral-rich lands.[24]

By the first years of the twentieth century, Consolidation Coal was ready to expand beyond the confines of western Maryland. According to a 1926 company history, Consolidation purchased the Millholland coalfield, near Morgantown, West Virginia, in 1902. Additional acquisitions were made in 1903, including the purchase of the Fairmont Coal Company of West Virginia and the Somerset Coal Company of Pennsylvania. These "purchases" were in no way the simple transactions the term suggests. With respect to the Fairmont Coal Company, for example, historians Richard B. Drake and John Alexander Williams note that Maryland and West Virginia entered into an interstate agreement that permitted Consolidation Coal to "absorb" the Fairmont Coal Company, headed by Clarence Watson (fig. 2.1). After Consolidation absorbed Fairmont Coal, Watson relocated to Baltimore, where he took control of Consolidation Coal. Mergers such as these permitted Consolidation to increase production significantly, from approximately 1.3 million tons in 1900 to 8.4 million tons in 1903.[25]

In 1909 the company moved into the Kentucky coalfields, acquiring thirty thousand acres of land in Johnson and Martin Counties, known as the Millers Creek field and, one year later, one hundred thousand acres of land in Pike, Letcher, and Knott Counties, known as the Elkhorn field.

Writing for the company's *Mutual Magazine* in 1928, Ewing G. Wells reasoned that credit for the acquisition of the Millers Creek field lay at the doorstep of one man:

> It is to Mr. John C. C. Mayo, who was teaching school where Consolidation Coal Company Mine Tipple No. 152 now stands that credit is given for first realizing the great possibilities that were to be had on a large scale in the coal business of the Van Lear section. Mr. Mayo knew of the openings on the Bowe Farm, the Webb Farm, and the Burgess Farm and that they were all located on the waters of Millers' Creek. He realized too, the exceptional qualities of this coal for domestic purposes. Not even the trying times of the financial panic in 1893 could weaken Mr. Mayo's faith in the great possibilities for coal development in this field and all through the period of the panic he went about buying and selling mineral properties to prospective operators, hoping to induce capital to enter this field that was certain to be pierced by the coming railroad. . . . The Consolidation Coal Company, through Senator C. W. Watson and his associates, purchased large tracts of acreage in this territory from Mr. Mayo in 1907 and their good judgment was not long in being proved by the remarkable development which got under way soon afterward in this division.

Fig. 2.1. "Clarence W. Watson, President of Consolidation Coal Company 1903–1911 and 1919–1928, Chairman 1911–1919." Watson presided over the company's tremendous growth during the first three decades of the twentieth century.

This spirited chronicle of the company's past is revealing for at least two reasons. First, we are made aware of the value Consolidation Coal affixed to telling its own "heroic" story and instilling a sense of pride among employers and employees alike. Second, we are reminded of the pedestal upon which individuals like Mayo, Watson, and others were placed, by company promoters but perhaps also by a larger segment of American society. That men like Mayo, Clarence Watson, and Aretas B. Fleming were held up as near mythic figures in company literature says much about their power and influence. In a biographical sketch of Clarence Watson—published on the occasion of his retirement from the presidency of Consolidation Coal—one contributor to the *Mutual Monthly* wrote, "Senator Watson, his older brothers and his father before him were great business men, great organizers and great developers. The coal industry in northern West Virginia was practically brought into being by them, began to be important with them, and for more than two generations had the benefit of their guidance and management."[26]

As Consolidation Coal's holdings grew by leaps and bounds on the map, so too did the power wielded by the region's coal and railroad barons. The emergence of the so-called Fairmont Ring in West Virginia serves as a case in point. The ring, as Harry Caudill dubbed it, included, among others, Peter H. Watson of the B&O Railroad, Johnson N. Camden of the Monongahela Coal and Coke Company and John D. Rockefeller's right arm at Standard Oil, and Clarence W. Watson of the Fairmont Coal Company. Aretas B. Fleming, attorney for the B&O and Standard Oil and former governor of West Virginia, is generally credited with bringing them all together under the umbrella of Consolidation Coal. Thanks to allies like Mayo, whose reputation for acquiring valuable coal lands by any means necessary was legendary, the Fairmont Ring extended Consolidation's already considerable reach into the Elkhorn and Millers Creek fields of Kentucky. The fact that many of these moguls also held political office shows the extent to which local, state, and national politics, financial institutions, the railroads, and King Coal were intimately tied to one another during this era. Indeed, both Johnson Camden, representing Kentucky in the U.S. Senate, and Clarence Watson, serving West Virginia in the same capacity, occupied positions that enabled them to formulate policies that favored the very industry that had made them wealthy.[27]

By 1917, Consolidation Coal operated 107 mines and controlled approximately 303,000 acres of coal and timber lands in four Appalachian states. Of this total, 13 mines and 14,000 acres were situated in Allegany County, Maryland; 25 mines and 58,000 acres in Somerset County, Pennsylvania; 50 mines and 100,000 acres in Barbour, Harrison, Marion, and Monongalia Counties in West Virginia; and 19 mines and 131,000 acres in Johnson, Knott, Letcher, and Pike Counties in Kentucky. About this same time, in 1915, the Rockefeller family purchased their first stock in the Consolidation Coal Company. Soon thereafter they came to control 38 percent of the securities of the company.[28]

In 1927, Consolidation became the largest commercial producer of bituminous coal in the United States. In that year, the company operated ninety-two mines, employed over twelve thousand workers representing forty-three nationalities, and possessed an estimated 2.7 billion net tons of unmined mineral resources. In 1864—the company's first full year of production—Consolidation shipped 37,678 tons of coal from its mines in western Maryland—an amount, writes company historian C. L. Green in 1927, that could be loaded on four modern coal trains. In 1927, nearly thirteen million tons of coal were removed from the company's principal properties: the Elkhorn and Millers Creek Divisions of Kentucky; the Fairmont Division of West Virginia; Pennsylvania's Somerset and Jenner mines; and the Georges Creek Division of Maryland.[29]

The late 1920s and the 1930s brought declining sales, depressed wages, labor unrest, and, for many connected with the coal industry, financial ruin. According to one source, "Like a series of mine explosions, the failure of coal corporations and banks swept away the economic structure." For industry giant Consolidation Coal, the 1930s brought a 40 percent decline in production and, in 1932, bankruptcy. It was at this time that the Rockefeller interests in the company took a huge loss, at which point they "retired from the coal scene." Receivership, reorganization, and recovery followed on the heels of financial collapse. As difficult as these times were for Consolidation Coal, a recent company history placed the episode in the best possible light: "Through sacrifices and hard work from everyone, Consol rallied and continued on. By its seventieth birthday in 1934, production climbed back to 9.8 million tons, and it had become the world's foremost producer of bituminous coal. . . . It had more than 1.8 billion tons of reserves and 22 operating mines in Maryland, Pennsylvania, West Virginia and Kentucky."[30]

During the 1940s and 1950s, according to Duane Smith, the coal mining industry, "confronted by the decades-old competition from oil and natural gas, receded to a mere shadow of its former national significance." Nevertheless, the Second World War did give the industry a much-needed boost, albeit a temporary one. During the war and soon thereafter, Consolidation acquired additional properties in northern West Virginia, as well as in Ohio. Ironically, at the same time that the company was expanding into these new areas, it was withdrawing from the state where it had first left its mark. In March 1944, eight decades after its first shipment of coal rolled east toward Baltimore, Consolidation Coal leased or sold its remaining properties in the Georges Creek valley. Just over eighteen months later, in November 1945, Pittsburgh Coal and Consolidation Coal—at the time the two largest commercial coal companies in the country—combined to form the behemoth Pittsburgh Consolidation Coal Company.[31]

Consolidation's history since the merger with Pittsburgh Coal—including its transition to highly mechanized surface mining, its attempts at diversification, its emphasis on providing feedstock for coal-fired power plants, and, later, its acquisition by the Continental Oil Company (Conoco) and affiliation with DuPont—reflects the changes the coal industry has undergone in general over the last fifty years. Of particular interest to us, however, is a more obscure event: the sale in 1956 of most of the company's large holdings in the Elkhorn field in Kentucky to the Beth-Elkhorn Corporation, for it was Beth-Elkhorn that came into possession of a remarkable collection of coal-mining photographs.[32]

Images of the Company Town

I am the man that mines the coal,
That digs and tunnels like the mole,
That loads and hauls and dumps and screens
And works for nothing—so it seems.

—"The Coal Operator," 1931

Contrasting Views

In 1965 Presbyterian minister Jack E. Weller published a sobering assessment of life in West Virginia's mountains. *Yesterday's People* reflects on the author's thirteen years as a missionary in various small communities throughout the Mountaineer State. The picture he paints of central Appalachia—its towns and its inhabitants—during the middle years of the twentieth century is not a flattering one. His grim, powerful description of the dilapidated coal company towns that dot the countryside, for instance, is characteristic of the book's tone:

The middle class traveler, as he journeys through rural Appalachia, is not likely to be favorably impressed with much that he sees. He will observe rows of coal-camp houses with peeling paint; elsewhere, unpainted, weather-stained houses set on blocks or posts (allowing chickens or house pets some shelter and escape), perched on the hillsides or back from the creek banks; the front porch with its ever occupied rocking chairs or a swing, and children everywhere.

In the visitor's eyes the well-kept garden patches and the picturesque narrow footbridges swinging precariously across the creeks
in front of the houses cannot make up for the dumps of trash
spread everywhere.

Weller's observations, reinforced over the years by the news media and
popular press, have left us with a decidedly negative image of coal camps
and company towns in Appalachia. As David H. Mould observes, the
company town, more often than not, is seen as a "blemish on the landscape," a place where we find "decaying frame houses" and "primitive
working conditions," a place where "economic servitude breeds dreary
architecture and dreary lives."[1]

Turn the clock back forty years from the publication of Weller's book
and peruse the pages of Consolidation Coal's photo albums or, alterna-
tively, the pages of the company's periodical, the *CCC Mutual Monthly
Magazine,* and one is left with a decidedly different—an almost won-
drous—impression of these once teeming centers of industrial activity. The
following description of Jenkins, Kentucky, from 1927 is representative:

I had ridden and bounced over the rails for a day and a half to
reach the land of my dreams. Someone told me that sixteen years
ago a group of far-seeing business men rode into this primitive
Kentucky valley and settled down to the task of giving Elkhorn
coal to the world. Their first job was to bring in supplies, then cut
lumber, build houses and make a livable, two-fisted American community. It seemed incredible that this firmly established, steady settlement had been built in those short years. By looking up and
down the road it was possible to see much of the community with
its practically new store, warehouse, meat market, ice plant, bakery, power generating plant, hospital, schools, and churches. It has
all the appearance of an old, well regulated, firmly established,
self-sustaining center of population.

The difference between Weller's description and that found in the *Mutual
Monthly* can, of course, be explained easily enough. By the 1960s, Appalachia's once thriving coal economy was reeling. Taken together, overexpan-
sion, conflict between management and labor, mechanization, and, later,
competition from Western mines, new environmental regulations, and an
insatiable national appetite for oil and natural gas had greatly reduced the
size of the industry's workforce. Even as early as the 1920s the industry was
showing signs of distress. For many coal companies, the first shock waves

of depression preceded the stock market crash of 1929 by several years. Across Appalachia, the economic, social, and environmental effects were devastating. Moreover, the changes brought about were permanent. By the time Weller sat down to pen *Yesterday's People*, coal mining's halcyon days had long since passed.[2]

The company town is one of the most important features associated with Appalachia's coal-mining regions. Simply stated, a company town is "a geographical location where a company establishes an economic activity and provides housing for its workers." Once a coal company purchased or leased land and mineral rights in an area and then constructed a railroad link, the job of hiring and housing workers and commencing mining operations could begin. The importance of establishing a reliable transportation link between mineral-producing areas and crucial Eastern markets cannot be overstated. As historian Richard B. Drake points out, coming up with the necessary capital and spreading the financial risk among major players was also an important consideration:

> The expenditure of funds, human blood, and energy that had built the railways into the hitherto remote mountain areas of Appalachia is legendary. Whether in West Virginia, . . . or in North Carolina, or Kentucky, the per-mile cost of building these railroads in dollars and human lives is staggering. And so great was the financial risk in opening a new coalfield in a remote mountain area that the resources of great rail companies, such as the Louisville and Nashville and the Chesapeake and Ohio, had to be combined with those of great energy corporations, such as the Consolidation Coal Company of Maryland.

Because large exploitable seams of coal in central and southern Appalachia were often located in remote areas, labor had to be imported from elsewhere. Thus the need to provide housing and other amenities for workers and their families. Company towns were especially important features in southern Appalachia, where during the 1920s an estimated two-thirds to three-fourths of all miners in eastern Kentucky, southern West Virginia, and southwestern Virginia lived in such settlements. According to David Alan Corbin, the figure for southern West Virginia alone approached 98 percent. By the 1950s company towns had all but faded from the scene.[3]

The literature dealing with the company town is extensive and, to some extent, contradictory. While some scholars have maintained that the "grasping company image" has been exaggerated and that many companies treated their employees with both respect and fairness, others—and, it would seem, the majority—have argued that company-owned towns, while perhaps a necessity in the initial stages of mine development, permitted companies to exert an objectionable level of control over the lives of their employees:

> Since the camp's existence is entirely dependent upon the mine, its whole life revolves around the routine of the whistles, the shifts, the trains, and the tipple. Life as it was lived in the traditional coal camp would strike most of us as strange indeed. Because the company owned the whole community, the community danced to the tune of the company's pipe. The miner and his family, if they went to church, did so in a building provided by the company and heard a preacher who was selected and hired by the company and often paid through a compulsory checkoff system before the men received their wages. The school building was often provided by the company and so was the teacher. The store was a company store and bound the miners to it through a system of scrip, which was really an advance on next pay day's money. . . . If there were movies in town, they were shown in a company-provided building. Water, electricity, coal, and garbage collection (if any) were provided by the company at token cost. If any community improvements were made—sidewalks, recreation fields, road maintenance—they were usually initiated and carried out by the company. Thus, the company did not train, and did not intend to train, the individualistic mountaineer in forms of community organization. Management told him what needed to be done, and, in total dependence, the miner did what he was told.

Considering the degree to which some companies monitored social life, manipulated local news media and politics, controlled local law enforcement, and dominated educational and religious institutions, corporate influence was even more far reaching than Weller's account would have us believe. But the establishment of these mining communities was symbolic of an even greater shift in social relations. As historian Ronald D. Eller observed twenty years ago, "the mining towns also reflected the underlying transition in land ownership and social power which had swept the region with the coming of the industrial age." While they performed a valuable function at the outset, in the end this arrangement—in some places at least—ushered in an era of bitter, sometimes violent, relations between management and labor. As Eller eloquently put it, "[W]hen they were abandoned by their creators to die and decay in the depression days of the late 1920s, the company towns came to represent in the popular mind the tragic dilemma of Appalachia itself."[4]

The Consolidation Coal Town

Like other companies, Consolidation Coal constructed towns for its workers (figs. 3.1–2). Unlike many other companies, Consolidation's towns often included schools, churches, hospitals, post offices, recreational buildings, and general stores. The company even constructed ballparks and sponsored baseball leagues (fig. 3.3). The games, which pitted local mining towns against one another, were often very competitive, as the following report from two West Virginia towns indicates: "Considerable rivalry has been stirred up in the past two weeks between the baseball teams at Mines Nos. 86 and 87. The season opened Sunday, April 27th, at Ida May with a game between Carolina and Ida May, resulting in a score of 5 to 4 in favor of Ida May. Both teams are anxious to hear from other Consolidation teams to arrange games, none being barred."[5]

Consol's efforts to construct substantial towns with at least some amenities were recognized by the Kentucky Geological Survey in 1927. According to Willard Rouse Jillson of the survey,

> The layout of a new mining camp from a practical standpoint has generally been dependent upon the type of organization which has come into the field, the thickness of the coal proposed to operate, and the area to be developed. Where these factors have been of sufficient size to warrant it, excellent operations laid out according to the best mining and sanitary practice have been installed. Such operations are to be found at Jenkins, McRoberts and Fleming, in Letcher county. In these localities, high type camps have been developed with water and sewage systems, amusements, hospital facilities, grade and high schools, and paved streets. Welfare work has been undertaken, and a great deal of stress has been laid on securing the best possible living conditions consistent with efficient coal mining operation.

As Jillson's report implies, these towns (Jenkins, McRoberts, and Fleming were Consolidation towns) stood apart from other coal-mining settlements in Kentucky. They were, in effect, model towns. One contributor to the

Fig. 3.1. "Miners' Houses Owings Mine Dec. 2, 1909."

Fig. 3.2. "Miners Houses Consolidation No. 32 Mine Sep. 5, 1910."

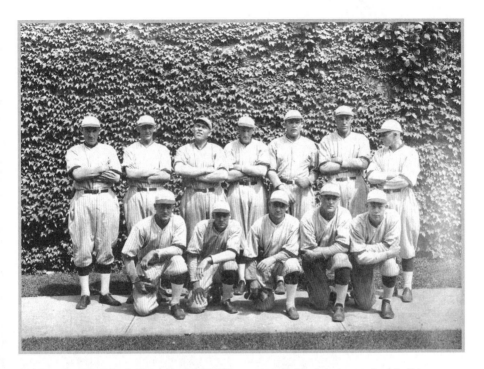

Fig. 3.3. "Jenkins Baseball team—7-4-23." Many mines fielded their own baseball teams.

magazine in 1926 remarked, "Jenkins is a town worth living in, is the boast of new citizens as well as old ones. . . . The scenery is lovely, the lake affords such pleasures as boating and fishing. The well kept lawns and beautiful flowers are added attractions. Automobile riding is now a pleasure as the roads have been repaired and oiled and are free from dust" (fig. 3.4).[6]

In addition to building lasting towns for its workers, Consolidation also sought to improve conditions in its older towns, as well as in the towns it acquired through purchase from other companies, as the following dispatches to the *Mutual Monthly* from 1922 to 1926 demonstrate:

> This is our first contribution to the C.C.C. Mutual Monthly Magazine, and due to the short time which we have had to gather the happenings, our article must be very brief. We have only been employees of The Consolidation Coal Company since February 13th. We are very much pleased with the interest shown in our living conditions and hope that our town will be made to look quite different within the near future.
>
> The appearance of Jenners [Jenner mine in Pennsylvania] has been greatly changed since the painters have completed the work of

Fig. 3.4. "Mud Town Street, looking up hill." Not all mining communities enjoyed the advantage of paved roadways.

painting the houses. The old custom of one color for all houses has been changed to various combinations which adds materially to the bright and cheery looks of the town.

Bell is being rapidly improved. The streets have been graded, ditches cleaned and tilted at many places, and sidewalks built around the mine and tipple. Grading has been started to beautify the lawns around the Recreation Building, store and mine office. Garbage is being disposed of and the miners' houses repaired.

We are glad to note that Monongah mines are included in the Coal Company's improvement program for better houses and general conditions of our miners. Work is already progressing in cleaning up about the house plant, tearing down old buildings and making general repairs to houses.

A programme of development, approved by the Executive
Committee of our Company in July calls for the expenditure of
vast sums of money upon improvements designed to provide an
immediate increase in production of more than a hundred per cent
for their mines of the Fairmont Field. A separate programme of
improvements, affecting living conditions of their mine workers,
which involves the expenditure of hundreds of thousands of dollars
upon renovating existing houses, removing others, and building
a large number of houses, has also been approved by the committee. . . . Some of the older mining towns will be practically rebuilt,
old buildings will be replaced by new ones. Roads will be built and
improved and sidewalks and fences built. Drainage and other conditions affecting sanitation will be improved. Electric lights and running water will be installed and hundreds of new houses will be
built for miners.

As the foregoing passages plainly show, Consolidation invested significant
time and money into refurbishing many of its properties. The expenditure was justified on the grounds that such measures helped to preserve
the property and that a healthy workforce was a more productive workforce, a sentiment freely expressed by company officials, who argued that
"old dilapidated and unsightly shacks and buildings" not only detracted
from the appearance of towns but were also "a menace to health." Insist-
ing that many of these buildings were improperly constructed to begin
with and that many were being used for housing chickens, pigs, cows, and
other animals, one official, Hugh Griffin, recommended their removal to
avoid creating "foul and unsanitary surroundings."[7]

Even if exaggerated somewhat, the balance of evidence suggests that
the Consolidation Coal Company invested more time and money than
other companies when it came to construction and upkeep of their towns.
Returning to Jillson's report for the geological survey:

As contrasted to such splendid mining town equipment, there
exists generally throughout the Eastern Coal Field a more haphaz-
ard and unsystematized layout of coal operations. In the small
camps, houses are poorly constructed with little or no attention
paid to their architecture or usefulness. Sanitation is neglected, and
an adequate pure water supply is a rare thing. Clean amusements
and modern hospital facilities are generally given no thought at all,

and the condition of the roads or the schools is left to the county authorities with the result that in most cases neither are provided to serve the mining community.

Eller writes that by 1925, "living conditions in the mining camps of the southern mountains were among the worst in the nation." Historian Jerry Bruce Thomas discloses how economic decline during the 1920s and 1930s caused conditions in many such towns to deteriorate—conditions that, for many, were already poor to begin with.[8]

How can we account for the great disparity in work and living conditions that might distinguish one company's towns from those of another? According to Margaret M. Mulrooney, several factors influenced the degree to which a coal operator would invest time and money in the development of a town. These included the number of houses that had to be built, the projected life of the mine, and the amount of capital available. In the case of Consolidation Coal, there was also a firm belief in the interlocking principles of contentment sociology, welfare capitalism, corporate paternalism, and industrial Americanism. Well-built towns offering a wide range of amenities and entertainments attracted a more dependable and loyal breed of miner. A contented worker well satisfied with conditions at home and in the workplace would reject all overtures from union organizers and communist sympathizers, or so the thinking went. In historian John C. Hennen's estimation, "Welfare capitalism was a prime ingredient in the recipe for employer control over production, efforts to thwart unionism, and the creation of an obedient, content, and thrifty working class."[9]

As Crandall Shifflett reminds us, however, many miners' families—especially the first generation to leave the farm—preferred life in the company town to the world they left behind or, in some cases, the world they had been forced to abandon. In a very real sense, they occupied a middle ground between life on the farm and life in crowded urban industrial centers:

> Contrary to the views that the coal mines and company controlled towns led to social fragmentation, disaffection, and alienation of the workforce, many miners and their families found life in them to be a great improvement over the past. Miners viewed the company town, not in comparison to some idyllic world of freedom, independence and harmony, but against the backdrop of small farms on rocky hillsides of Tennessee, Kentucky, and Virginia, or a sharecropper's life in the deep South states.

Similarly, sociologist Alan Banks points out that some coal operators looked upon their creations with pride: "They believed that their company towns were superior to anything found in the surrounding countryside. In the midst of what they perceived as barren wilderness, entire cities were built, sometimes complete with spacious homes, electricity, bath houses, parks, and hotels."[10]

But the company's motives were, in reality, more self-serving, for "the real value of company towns was not so much in the lavish accommodations provided for workers but in the fact that the social organization of the company solved real problems." By providing housing, company officials knew that the threat of eviction strengthened their hand when it came to relations between management and labor. By equating union activity with communist sympathy and, just as important, loyalty to the company with patriotism and "Americanism," they played on the vulnerabilities of foreign-born workers. Suffice it to say that the images in this chapter can only be understood if we remind ourselves of the historical context within which they were made.[11]

In this chapter, we will consider images associated with town layout and design, the company store, cultural diversity, the miner's garden, and health and sanitation. In so doing, we will focus on the ideas and messages the company sought to communicate to investors, employees, and the general public through the medium of photographs. We will also identify those aspects of company town life that are noticeably absent or difficult to read in the company's albums and publications. Even though the photographs in this chapter show scenes from just one company's towns, they are, nevertheless, representative of company town landscapes found across Appalachia and, perhaps to a great extent, across other parts of the United States as well between 1880 and 1930.[12]

Town Layout and Design

In her article on the coal company towns of southwestern Pennsylvania, Margaret Mulrooney identified five distinguishing characteristics of the coal company town—characteristics that are easily discernible in the Smithsonian collection of photographs. First and foremost, she noted that these towns were typically "financed, built, owned, maintained, and operated" by just one company. Everything in the town—houses, schools, churches, hospitals, stores, and ballparks—was provided by the company and, more often than not, bore the stamp of the company engineer as opposed to the architect. Thus the power of a single corporate entity—

Fig. 3.5. "Houses Lower Wrights Fork 5/6/13."

Fig. 3.6. "Street in West Jenkins, May 19, 1912."

Fig. 3.7. "Portable Houses—Dunham."

generally headquartered outside the region—might be largely responsible for the cultural landscapes created in a given area. With regard to the "built" environment, it is worth noting that by 1926 Consolidation Coal had 7,474 dwelling houses, thirty-six stores, seventeen recreation buildings, twenty-three equipped playgrounds, and two clubhouses.[13]

A second characteristic feature of the company town is that the dominant house type was a one- or two-story detached dwelling, each identical to the next in terms of style and construction. Looking at figures 3.5 and 3.6, we see that wood was the primary construction material, and further, that balloon-frame construction techniques, along with simplified Georgian and Victorian styles, produced a landscape of simplicity and uniformity. Although the emphasis was clearly on these two key themes, examples of architectural variation can be found in the collection. In contrast to miners' dwellings owned by other companies, Consolidation's were often—but not always—plastered throughout and equipped with running water and electricity.[14]

In later years, prefabricated and portable houses were also constructed, which leads us to a third trait of the company town—economy of construction (fig. 3.7). Recognizing that these mining communities

Fig. 3.8. "COMPANY BOARDING HOUSE—GYPSY." Boardinghouses were more closely associated with early mine development than with more firmly established operations.

were unlikely to develop into permanent settlements, coal operators limited their initial investment in housing so as to minimize financial loss when mining operations ceased. By charging workers rent, the cost of construction was often recovered quickly. The type of housing we find in a company town can tell us much about the miners employed there. Both Mulrooney and Shifflett argue that coal operators were particularly interested in hiring married men with families, noting that family men would be "less inclined to pick up and leave." Thus the three- and four-room single-family dwelling was favored over the large boardinghouse or tenement as the most common type of dwelling, although examples of the latter are to be found in the collection (fig. 3.8). Chronologically speaking, the shift from boardinghouse to detached dwelling and from a labor force dominated by single males to one increasingly made up of married men signals the transition from the more rudimentary coal camp to the more firmly established and community-oriented coal town.[15]

A standard pattern of town layout and settlement is the fourth fea-

Fig. 3.9. "Railroad depot at Fleming, Kentucky." Standardized housing and a linear pattern of development are evident in this photograph taken 19 November 1915.

ture. The typical company town was arranged in a linear or gridlike pattern, with miners' houses sited at the front of long, narrow lots and lined up along railroad routes or creek beds (figs. 3.9–10). These dwellings were generally clustered near the mine opening so miners could walk to work. Company historian Charles Beachley observed that towns were often situated this way because of the "narrowness of the valleys and the steepness of the hillsides," which "rendered the problem of locating houses most perplexing." Especially apparent is the extent to which the company town was centrally planned and standardized, reflecting the control wielded by the company's engineering department. Of course, not all company towns in the United States exhibit such a high degree of regularity. As geographer Richard Francaviglia has shown, rugged terrain could force street layouts to deviate from the grid pattern and follow the contours of the land. In

Fig. 3.10. "View of Jenkins from Raven Rock 7-5-23." Finding level ground on which to build a town often proved challenging.

Fig. 3.11. "House Superintendents Mine 21."

the case of some especially large operations with several mines, especially in the American West, company towns were divided into several sister communities, consisting of different nodes of activity.[16]

A fifth characteristic is differentiation, exhibited as an outward expression of socioeconomic stratification, with distinct gradations of wealth and power manifested on the landscape (figs. 3.11–12). Most conspicuous are the differences in housing and living conditions between the miners and their families and the coal operators and their managers, presenting the image of a bimodal society sharply divided between management and labor. Segregation according to racial and ethnic group was also common. Although the point will be taken up later in this chapter, it is worth noting that some coal companies sought to play whites, blacks, and immigrants off against one another as a means by which to stave off efforts to unionize the workforce.[17]

The Company Store

One of the more prominent and frequently photographed structures found in the coal mining town was the company store. According to

Fig. 3.12. "Manager's Residence." This view of the manager's residence in Jenkins, Kentucky, stands in sharp contrast to earlier photographs depicting miners' houses.

Francaviglia, the typical company store "was a rather large building that housed many different departments; it was, in effect, a large general store. Some, especially those in larger communities, occupied an entire city block" (fig. 3.13). Usually located beside the railroad tracks, the company store could exhibit a wide range of architectural styles, from simple utilitarian to the highly ornate. In addition to providing essentials such as food and clothing, the store sold mining supplies, tools for the garden, durable household goods, tobacco, and sundry items. With administrative offices situated on the upper floors, the store was also the "official arm" of the company.[18]

The following tour of the Jenkins Store in Kentucky, featured in the *Mutual Monthly* in 1927, gives us a feel for what one might expect to find upon entering a company store in one of Consolidation Coal's "model towns." The interior depicted in figure 3.14, meanwhile, provides us with valuable imagery. The description of the Jenkins store is particularly noteworthy for its exuberant endorsement of the store's merchandise and layout. According to the contributor of the piece:

Fig. 3.13. "McRoberts Store." The company store was often the largest building in town.

You would not expect to find an establishment like this in the hills of Kentucky. It is big and airy. The merchandise is shown to the very best advantage. Along one side of the first floor are men's furnishings, hats, and clothing, nationally advertised lines. Nothing too good for our employees at Jenkins; just the kind of trappings that every fellow enjoys strutting in. In the rear is the grocery department. All of the well known standard package and canned goods are on the shelves. On the other side are books, cigars, and supplies. These supplies include perfumes from France, pottery from the kilns of Japan, and intricately etched brass work from India. In the center of the floor is an island piled high with sweets and pastries from our own ovens. . . . The front wall of these rooms is a complete glassed-in show window ten feet high.

Then it is on to the second floor:

Tucked away in one corner is the milliner's work room and a stock room. Our Jenkins women can surely wear some "crowns" if this stockroom gets in its work. The third floor is given over to furniture. Anything from an inexpensive kitchen chair and "parlor

Fig. 3.14. "Men's Furnishings Dept. Jenkins Store."

suites" to washing machines. But the real hit of the store from the standpoint of community service and ability is the bargain basement. Here are over five hundred items of all descriptions, razor blades, mop pails, umbrellas, radio supplies, tools, nails, dishware, and I don't know what all, ranging from a few cents to a dollar.

Unfortunately, the company store was not the neutral retail space that photographers and magazine editors made them out to be. In reality, the company store was a far more complex institution; one in which many of the best and worst aspects of company town life came together.[19]

Especially in smaller towns, the company store doubled as meeting house, lodge, recreation hall, and, in some cases, even housed the post office. In this way, it was an important gathering place where people could exchange information in an informal setting. As Crandall Shifflett reminds us:

No other place in the company town brought as many people together in one location. Certainly not the churches, which were not well attended. The lodges, ballfields, dance halls, and other places of leisure and amusement, just like the church, attracted people, but these were planned encounters with a purpose, not the chance meetings of a variety of town folk across social, ethnic, and racial lines. . . . If there was one spot in the town to relieve boredom, one theater of uncertainty and mystery, one imaginary connection to faraway places, it would have been the place where the trains arrived and departed, bringing with them passengers and freight. Such was the case even for management.

As Shifflett is quick to point out, however, friendships extending across class lines were probably rare, especially when one takes into account that many stores were segregated. It is also unlikely that all the store's patrons were treated as equals. Indeed, evidence suggests that Consolidation Coal experienced its share of complaints over discriminatory practices at some of its stores. In reviewing a list of grievances registered with company officials in 1926, F. R. Lyon, vice president of operations, stated that twenty-one people complained of discourtesy, twelve of racial discrimination, ten of short weights in the meat markets, nineteen of slow service, four complained that certain goods were not in stock, seven complained about the quality of merchandise sold, and "one customer complained about the milk." By far the greatest number of complaints involved the price of items at the company store. According to Lyon, "The few complaints about charge accounts, deliveries, errors in charging and religious discrimination show that these are not serious defects." Similarly, Lyon brushed off allegations of racial discrimination. Noting that "eight colored people complained they were not given service in turn and four whites complained they were not given as good service as colored people," he concluded: "The fact that each side complains that the other is favored may indicate that both are being treated fairly." Given the unequal status accorded African Americans and immigrants from southern and eastern Europe at this time, Lyon's conclusion is hardly convincing.[20]

As the preceding paragraph clearly shows, residents were not always satisfied with the goods or services provided by the company store. While mining towns developed by entrepreneurs and speculators might offer a choice of places to shop, towns controlled by a single mining enterprise often did not. In some cases, the mining company forbade the establishment of other commercial retail operations altogether. Access to the railroad, a captive supply of customers, and a remote location—at least in the early stages of mine development—all worked to the advantage of the company. Taking these factors into consideration, it is not surprising that charges of debt peonage, coercion, price gouging, and differential pricing were leveled at the mining company.[21]

The charge of debt peonage is an important one. Considering that company employees were often paid in scrip—a form of currency issued by the company that could only be redeemed in merchandise at the company store—the danger of accumulating substantial debt was a real one and some miners, no doubt, fell into this trap. Shifflett maintains, however, that debt peonage was relatively rare and that most miners avoided "owing their souls to the company store," an impressive feat given the low wages some families were required to live on. At any rate, by the 1940s Consol was phasing out the use of scrip, as this announcement affirms:

> With the current change wherein scrip is being discontinued, the communities of Jenkins, McRoberts, and Van Lear take one more step away from a company town set-up. During July scrip issuance will be replaced at all Champion Stores by the normal credit system generally used by merchants throughout the country. Credit will thus continue to be available to Consol employees so desiring it but it will be on a more normal basis. Scrip had its day and served a good purpose in some respects, but it also had its evils and no tears need be shed over its passing.

It is also worth noting that miners were constantly encouraged, via the pages of the company magazine, to live frugally, avoid debt, and contribute regularly to a savings account. Nonetheless, Corbin charges that the company store was the "greatest drain on the miners' wages."[22]

Were operators guilty of coercing employees into trading at the company store? Certainly, in more remote areas where retail options were few, miners and their families were placed at a disadvantage. This was especially the case in instances where the mine operation was just getting started. In situations where other stores were available, however, evidence suggests that some companies were willing to employ heavyhanded tactics to ensure that their employees remained loyal patrons of the company store. In time, however, the company store evolved into a service that company officials used to entice employees, a particularly important asset in a tight labor market.[23]

With respect to pricing, there is strong evidence that companies—Consolidation Coal included—charged higher prices than other retail establishments. Some scholars have suggested that charging higher prices at the store was a deliberate policy designed to recoup losses associated with selling coal below the cost of production. The fact that Consolidation devoted space to the matter in the company magazine underscores the seriousness of the problem. In a short piece entitled "Our Merchandising Policy," C. S. Moss wrote that the company was working hard to address problems at the company stores. With regard to pricing, he remarked,

> Our old method of allowing all store managers to figure their own retail prices caused different stores to have different prices on the same article and we were often asked why the same article was priced differently in our different stores. Under the new system this trouble is partially eliminated as we have standard retail prices on groceries in all of our stores and are working toward a standard retail price on all items. This alone has done much toward gaining the good will of the Company employees.

Consolidation Coal's attempts to address shortcomings in the operation of its company stores did not stop there. In addition to standardizing prices and improving customer service, the company's "reorganization and general improvement" effort included carrying out physical improvements at stores throughout Kentucky, West Virginia, and Pennsylvania, and appointing, on 15 August 1927, a new general manager, Frank L. Parsloe of Brooklyn. In his former position, Parsloe had been sales manager for the H. C. Bohack Grocery Company, a chain with over four hundred stores in and around New York City. As the following statement by the company's assistant general manager of stores, F. S. Wilson, indicates, however, the new improvements did not win plaudits from everyone:

> Some of you are probably a little bit discouraged by the failure of some of our customers to believe in the sincerity of our efforts to give them better stores. We know that our stores are cleaner and better equipped than they were a year ago, a better variety of merchandise is offered for sale and the service is better. But some of our customers (fortunately only a few of them) still find nothing good about the stores.

Nevertheless, company officials continued to fight the public relations battle in the pages of the company journal, boasting of the quality of the company store's merchandise and the improved quality of service, expounding on the merits of shopping for items in person as opposed to using a mail order catalog, and, perhaps most important, attributing higher prices to the cost of transporting goods to remote locations.[24]

While debt peonage, coercion, and price gouging were not unheard of, by World War I, store managers could ill afford to alienate company workers, especially in the face of increased competition from mail-order houses, local stores, vendors, and other company stores. Even before other businesses arrived on the scene, residents could board the train and conduct at least some of their shopping in a larger town. According to Shifflett, the company store's "power and control over the mining population was blunted by the rational behavior of miners and the business acumen of company officials who understood the limits of their control in a tight labor market."[25]

Cultural Diversity

Yet another characteristic of the mining community—one not always easily discerned in the photographs—was a culturally diverse labor pool. Beginning in the 1890s, coal companies began to recruit labor heavily from southern and eastern Europe. When the First World War broke out, immigration from Europe plummeted, opening the door for increased numbers of African Americans to enter the mines. By 1920, European immigration rebounded somewhat, adding further to the mix. The result was that company towns developed into places of sharp contrasts where "facilities were built in keeping with the custom of segregation along racial and ethnic lines." Under such conditions it was not unusual for three towns to exist side by side in a single setting: an immigrant town, a Negro town, and an "American" town. As Shifflett reminds us, "More than towns, these were really communities with their separate facilities, organizations, customs, and social life."[26]

Reflecting on life in a company town owned by the Fairmont Coal Company in West Virginia during the late 1920s and early 1930s, African American miner Robert Armstead recently wrote: "Grant Town had three places where blacks could live: Inktom Hill, Black Bottom, and Grays Flats. Like most black communities in coal camps, they were either a long walk from the mine or were right next to the mine and the railroad tracks, where it was noisy and dirty." As Armstead's memoir reveals, the lines of racial and ethnic demarcation were sharp:

> When we went to the company store, or church, or to the Grille, we passed by the white kids' school in town. Theirs was a big two-story brick structure, built solidly with many pieces of playground equipment. Inside, they had radiator heat, water fountains and sinks, and electric lights. Our school had neither electricity nor running water. We had coal stoves, one outside toilet, and gravel for a playground. We did have one see-saw and one swing. Black kids always played on the black playground. We were forbidden to play with white kids on the white school playground, after school or in the summer.
>
> . . .
>
> Armed with the love of my family, I accepted segregation. We all did. Black children hiked back and forth from Black Bottom past the white school each day. That was in the 1930s, twenty years before the Supreme Court ruled that all public schools had to integrate. Students at our school brought their lunches in brown paper bags. Very few kids had fruit. Many unfortunates never had any lunch at all. They stood around and begged at lunch time. . . . All black children in our area attending pre-primer through eighth grade had to walk to the Grays Flats' school. There were no buses for them. These rules and policies forced black people with children to live very close to the mining towns or else give up on their children's education.[27]

While certain patterns associated with town layout and ethnic segregation can be inferred by reading the captions that correspond to the images in the Smithsonian collection (figs. 3.15–16), evidence of cultural diversity is more readily observed in numerous photographs of African American and "foreign" miners posing for the camera at work or with their families at any of a number of social gatherings (figs. 3.17–19). While examples of this sort can be drawn from the museum collection, a great many others can be found in the pages of the *Mutual Monthly*. In many cases, the photographs that appear in the magazine can also be found in the museum's archive. As the following examples demonstrate,

Fig. 3.15. "Old Colored School at Tom Biggs Branch. 10-6-21."

Fig. 3.16. "McRoberts Colored Recreation Bldg. 10-13-21."

the articles and notes contained in the company magazine also provide valuable detail concerning the nationalities of recent immigrants. As an indicator of cultural complexity in the company towns the *Mutual Monthly* deserves more than a desultory glance.

Language and religion are key components of the "cultural baggage" that accompany us wherever we go. One of the most obvious ways in which the editors of the *Mutual Monthly* remind us that a great many immigrants, particularly from southern and eastern Europe, resided in Consolidation's towns is that they sometimes printed articles in languages other than English. In 1918, for example, a short series on first aid appeared in English, Italian, and Polish. Similarly, a short piece in 1921 admonished readers—in English, Italian, Polish, Russian, Hungarian, Romanian, and Slovak—to place their "surplus money in a sound American savings bank," where "it will make more money for you, in the form of interest, every day in the year." This short bank promotion provides us with important information concerning the national origins of the company's labor force at the time. Another announcement, appearing in both English and Hungarian, is valuable not only because it indicates that a significant proportion of miners emigrated from Hungary but also because the power of the company, not to mention the vulnerabilities of the immigrant during wartime, is so obviously on display:

> On this page appears an announcement to Hungarian miners of which the following is a translation, which translation has been duly filed with the New York post office with the affidavit that is required by law: In any country when war commences, everybody belonging to the country of the enemy is interned. The United States has not done this. It will not intern Hungarians so long as they continue at work and make no trouble. No one who does his duty will lose his job. Everyone will be as well treated as if he were a citizen of the United States, so long as he behaves himself. He will not be deprived of his savings or his property. Hungarian miners have, therefore, reason to be grateful to the United States for its generosity. Hungarian miners can show their good will by working steadily and quietly. This nation and the mine owner heartily appreciate the services of those Hungarian miners who have labored steadily to get out a large quantity of clean coal.[28]

Perhaps no other passage so poignantly captures the image of a recent immigrant with little or no training in English as this one. Next to a picture accompanied by a caption that reads "A kindergarten class of

Fig. 3.17.
"Miner's Mine No. 48, 10-11-18."

Fig. 3.18. "4th July Celebration—Shoe Race, Col. 7-4-23."

Fig. 3.19. "4th July Celebration—Shoe Race, White 7-4-23."

C.C.C. children," the March 1918 issue of the *Mutual Monthly*
announced that the magazine would soon feature a section dedicated to
the entertainment of children called the John Martin Section:

> John Martin will make up a section of two pages each month just
> for you children, so tell your fathers to be sure to always bring this
> magazine right home so that you can see your part of it. The
> Magazine comes once each month so keep a lookout for it. Now
> some of you children have fathers and mothers who cannot read
> English, they read their own language, but have never studied
> English. You children should read the magazine to your parents. If
> you will read it to them they will enjoy the parts written for the
> grown-up folks just as much as you do the children's page.

Another photograph depicts an English-language class in session (fig.
3.20). Such images are rare in both the Smithsonian collection and the
Mutual Monthly. Occasionally, the magazine would carry news as well as
photographs of recent arrivals to town, as in the news from Mine No. 29
in West Virginia:

> Recently arrived at this mine, eight natives of Serbia, who,
> although then making their homes in this country, went back at
> the call of Patriotic Duty to fight for their homeland. Veterans of
> the World War; two of them wounded in this fierce struggle for
> World Dominion, discharged from the Serbian Army, their first
> thought was back to the good old U.S.A. Arriving in this country
> St. Patrick's Day, March 17, from Ragusa, Jugo-Slavonia, they
> were secured for our Company through the good offices of the
> Serbian Consul.[29]

Historian Ronald Lewis has shown that African Americans made up
a sizeable portion of the labor force in central Appalachia from approximately 1910 to the 1930s. Evidence also shows that Consol agents actively
recruited blacks to the mines, particularly to towns in eastern Kentucky
such as Jenkins, McRoberts, and Fleming. The *Mutual Monthly* provides
ample evidence of the vital role blacks played in Consolidation's towns in
Kentucky, Pennsylvania, and West Virginia. Nearly every issue contained
a section titled "Among Our Colored Folks," which brought readers up to
date, via stories and photographs, on the activities of African American
residents throughout the company's mining communities. In this way, the

Fig. 3.20. "Class in English Language, Jan. 25, 1913."

magazine's content and organization was a reflection of real life for the black miner—segregation was something to be encountered at every turn, even in the employee magazine. In 1918 the *Mutual Monthly* carried this stark reminder of the hierarchy blacks were subjected to at the time: "We colored people of Jenkins are faring well considering that the United States is at war, and if the white people continue to treat us as they have, the majority of us will be here for the better improving of Jenkins." The following description is illustrative of the "special events" often featured in the "Colored Folks" column (figs. 3.21–22):

> On August 9th, our colored people celebrated their Emancipation Day with a parade of floats, decorated automobiles, columns of children and a fine band. The day was spent in games and races. Prizes were awarded for the best decorated automobile and winners in races. Walter Bell, in his usual efficient manner, looked after the

barbecue of chickens, fish, porkers, and a beef. An orchestra was engaged for the occasion and a dance was given on the platform in the grove. The colored people came from all the adjoining towns and enjoyed the long-to-be-remembered day together.

More typical were notes on the comings and goings of various residents, birth announcements and death notices, and news from the schools, recreation halls, and the mines themselves—especially recognition of the month's champion coal loaders. There were also occasional references to blacks moving back to or visiting relatives in Alabama and Virginia—migrational patterns not uncommon to the period.[30]

Gary Farley and Bill Leonard write that one of the important amenities offered to mine workers was a church, often funded and constructed by the coal company (figs. 3.23–24):

> One or more might cater to the workers—Roman Catholic Italian, Polish, or Irish; Welch Baptist, Russian Orthodox, or German Lutheran. Another congregation—Presbyterian, Methodist, or Episcopal—was more likely to be provided for the management. In Central Appalachia, many of the miners were indigenous to the region, so the company might furnish a Baptist, Holiness, Methodist, or Presbyterian church for the workers.

Whether it was the construction of a new Slovak Catholic church at Mine No. 25 in West Virginia or an Italian Catholic church in Monongah, a photograph of the Mount Olive African Methodist Church or the Sunbeam Band Baptist Church, or the arrival of an itinerant preacher, news from the company's religious congregations was included in the *Mutual Monthly*. When, for instance, the new Russian Greek Orthodox church in Pine Hill, Pennsylvania, was formally dedicated on 11 August 1918, "the highest dignitary of the church in America, the Rt. Rev. Bishop Alexander of New York, who is the head of the diocese comprising the United States, Canada and Alaska," was on hand to perform the holy rites. At the conclusion of the dedicatory sermon, which was "preached . . . in the Russian language," a seven-course feast "prepared and served in Russian style" was served to those in attendance. The great variety of denominations is indicative of the religious diversity of Consol's workers.[31]

One of the more controversial aspects of coal company involvement in the establishment of churches is that ministers were paid in whole or in part by the companies. According to John C. Hennen, coal operators denied charges that building churches and paying ministers' salaries

Fig. 3.21. "Emancipation Day, 8-8-24."

Fig. 3.22. "Emancipation Day, 8-8-24."

Fig. 3.23. "Methodist Church at Jenkins, 3-4-30."

allowed them to exert even greater control in the company towns. The sermon "DIRTY COAL: Loading It Is Plain Dishonesty," reproduced in the pages of the *Mutual Monthly* in 1928, suggests otherwise:

"DIRTY COAL" [containing roof and/or floor rock and other impurities] was the subject chosen by Rev. B. Franklin Auld, pastor of the First Methodist Episcopal Church, recently. A large congregation, including many strange faces, gathered to hear this sermon. Extracts follow: 'Lonaconing [Maryland] is under the disadvantage of high production cost in mining coal, but she has the two advantages of high grade coal and high grade men. With her high grade men she can more than compete in the coal industry, but these men must apply themselves to the reduction of costs in mining. This they can do in saving wherever they can. All loss of materials and time finally hurts the miners. But they must also develop themselves through study at schools, so that they can become more efficient and quickly adopt the best methods. Furthermore, for their

Fig. 3.24. "Catholic Church, Jenkins."

own safety and the safety of their companions they should all
know how to apply first aid and how to use all precaution against
accidents. . . . The loading of "dirty" coal must be frowned upon.
To load dirty coal is plain dishonesty and hurts all the miners in
this section, because when a man once receives dirty coal from us he
will not buy from us again. Let us load clean coal and get a reputation not only for good coal, but for clean coal. . . . When we mine
clean coal we are proud of our product. We then can tell all the
world that our coal is the best. We can write to our friends wherever
they buy coal and we will be able to sell them our coal because it
is the best. This is the best kind of advertising. . . . We have not
mentioned the operator because we are now addressing miners. But
the operators can be depended upon for co-operation if the men set
about in adjustment of the coal industry in the spirit of the Master.

While the importance of religion in the coalfields should not be underesti-
mated, Weller and others have found that church attendance in the company

towns was relatively low and that competition among churches for parishioners was keen.[32]

Photographs of schoolchildren also provide us with valuable visual evidence of ethnic diversity—and segregation—in Consolidation Coal's towns (figs. 3.25–26). Here again, photographs cannot tell the whole story. While some have asserted that company-run schools carried corporate power and influence to new heights, company officials at the time argued that their involvement was absolutely necessary to ensure quality of education. According to Hennen, "An official for Consolidation Coal in Jenkins, Kentucky, explained that most mining companies tried to secure the most progressive teachers. Unless company officials took an interest in the selection of teachers, unconcerned board of education members would send their worst teachers to the mining towns." As this report from mines 50, 62, and 94 in West Virginia indicates, even company participation was not enough to ensure that schools could survive in isolated mining communities: "Owing to lack of funds to pay teachers, the school at this place closed about the middle of March, throwing the children out of school about a month or six weeks before the end of the regular term." These are points that do not rise to the surface in class photographs or images of happy children frolicking on the playground at recess.[33]

The Miner's Garden

Both the Smithsonian collection and the *Mutual Monthly* contain a surprisingly large number of photographs of vegetable and flower gardens. As was the case with other companies, Consolidation Coal encouraged its employees to plant gardens, both for food and as a means of beautifying the mining towns. The most common type of image was that of a garden contest winner posing in front of the prize-winning plot of ground. While acknowledging that "photographs cannot be made that will do justice to a garden," the editors of the company journal nevertheless endeavored to include as many images of contest winners as possible. The following entry from the *Mutual Monthly* is valuable not only for its reference to garden photography but for its description of mining town topography:

> Illustrations rarely do full justice to gardens, for, by reason of the topography of the average mining town, garden sites cannot be located to advantage for photographs. Many are on the sides of

Fig. 3.25. "Kindergarten—Foreign Class. 1921."

Fig. 3.26. "Colored School at Burdine."

hills so steep that one wonders how the seeds are prevented from rolling out of place before they germinate, others are in bottoms where they are hard to reach with the camera, others are so surrounded by buildings as to make it impossible to get good pictures of them. But in spite of all these handicaps they are real gardens, grown for the food they produce and not as fads or for the prizes offered.

This last comment notwithstanding, cash prizes were typically distributed among first-, second-, and third-place finishers. First-place winners from the individual communities then went on to compete at the divisional level. The Millers Creek Division Garden Contest for 1918 serves as an example. The prize for first place was twenty dollars, with fifteen, ten, and five dollars awarded for second, third, and fourth places respectively. Children's gardens were also judged. At stake were five-, three-, and two-dollar prizes. Young gardeners receiving honorable mention were given a book. As the photograph captions clearly indicate, separate prizes were issued to "white" and "colored" contestants (figs. 3.27–28). The names of winners were printed in the company monthly, accompanied by an image of the prize-winning garden. In some cases, the nationality of the winners was given. Of the twenty-one "white" winners in the West Virginia Division for 1923, for example, nine were identified as Americans, four as Italians, three as Slavish, three as Hungarian, and two as German, providing further proof of the cultural diversity prevalent in the company towns. Later, prizes were also disbursed to winners of flower competitions.[34]

Primary responsibility for the planting and care of the gardens appears to have rested on the shoulders of women and children, as the following passage indicates:

We are proud of our 1918 gardens, a record of several hundred, including the children's having been made; nor are the results due altogether to the season, but as much to the interest and work put into them, mostly by the women and children. The women of Van Lear [Kentucky] are no slackers. They have devoted hours, aye days, to garden making for the benefit of family and country. Many hours, that could have been leisure hours of rest or devoted to housework, have been cheerfully given to this good cause. There are instances where no garden would have been cultivated had it been left to the man of the family, for they have been busy mining

Fig. 3.27. "1st Prize Garden—Mine No. 201 8-17-26"

Fig. 3.28. "Ottis Harris, Col., Mine No. 203, 1st Pr., 8-26-23."

coal, but the industrious women stood behind the hoe, and wrestled from the soil enough wholesome food to last for almost the entire year; for in addition to the season's supply of all kinds of vegetables, gallons, pecks and bushels of fruits and vegetables have been taken care of for the non-growing season, when canned and dried products will be costly.

According to the company journal, the success of the gardens was due in part to the "very wise daylight saving law" which gave miners and their families "ample opportunity to work our gardens after the day's work had been finished."[35]

Given the emphasis placed on the planting of gardens by company officials, as measured by the space devoted to the topic in the *Mutual Monthly*, perhaps the number of garden photographs is not surprising after all. Many were taken during the First World War, when gardens were established to support the allied effort. As the following excerpt confirms, the company attached a sense of urgency to the planting of gardens by its employees, especially during the war years:

> By this time we hope that every employee of this company, who can possibly get a few square feet of ground, has a garden planted or at least ready for planting. The garden will be of more value this year to the owner than ever before, for with the railroads congested with coal, steel and other war necessities, they will not be able to handle the great quantities of fresh vegetables demanded by the public. And even were this not the case—if the railroads were able to transport the vegetables desired, farm-labor is so high, and men for farm work so scarce, that the prices would be prohibitive to the average man.

The author of another article maintained that the best way to deal with the crisis of clogged railroads brought on by the war was to "grow things for our table," the idea being that if miners' families themselves "raise the stuff we eat we'll help the railroad world to meet the troubles which beset it. The roads won't have to drag around this stuff we take from out the ground; we'll just step out and get it." In another editorial, the unsure footing of the coal industry was identified as a primary reason to establish and maintain a garden: "We wish to impress upon all our employees the importance of planting good gardens this year, for because of the unsettled conditions in industry gardens will have a relatively greater value than in normal times, and will, we feel sure, be greatly appreciated by those who have them." During the Great Depression many relief recipients were eventually required to cultivate gardens.[36]

In addition to battling "old man high cost of living," gardens—Victory Gardens, as they were sometimes referred to during the war years—were encouraged as a means of beautifying the company town:

> Gardening is carried on extensively and profitably in all of our divisions by our employees, almost without exception. During the past year great quantities of vegetables were raised, but the flowers were not neglected as photographic proofs will show. Hundreds of homes of our fellow workers were beautified, no other word describes them, with flowers. The stores, substations and other parts of the various operations were not lax in beautifying their surroundings. The photograph to the right at the top of this page illustrates what 25c worth of seed plus a little work will accomplish in beautifying a spot. To really appreciate this transformation one must remember that this particular spot was a cinder heap which would have taken a prize for ugliness.

The photograph of a substation adorned with flowers is just one of several that speak to the company's efforts to improve the appearance of its towns (fig. 3.29). To understand the logic behind the beautification effort, one has only to return to the tenets of contentment sociology: "To our minds these things are worth while for we believe that every man works better and is happier when working in pleasant surroundings."[37]

Company officials and citizens from Van Lear, Kentucky, seemed to have taken particular pride in their town's appearance:

> If you had visited Van Lear three or four years ago, and then happened to drop in this summer, you would notice a big difference in the appearance of the town, and this is not all due to the company, but more to the people themselves. They are keeping their places cleaner, taking more interest in their gardens and yards, and endeavoring to assist in every way to make living conditions as good as possible. We, all of us, who have been out and around different mining towns, know that there are few that compare favorably with Van Lear. Almost all the miners concede this, but we must make it better, and this can only be done by co-operation between employees and employer. The people must look after their

Fig. 3.29. "Flower Beds at No. 212 Substation. 1920."

homes, keep their yards and gardens clean and turn over all garbage to the garbage wagon. If this is done and no refuse thrown into the streets, it will be a very easy matter to keep the town clean and beautiful.

To promote better living conditions, prizes were soon awarded for a new contest, Best Kept Premises.[38]

How popular were these garden contests? In terms of sheer numbers of spectators, the turnout rivaled that of annual Christmas celebrations. According to the *Mutual Monthly,* the largest community gathering ever in Jenkins, Kentucky, took place in 1919, when over eight hundred people attended the garden awards ceremony. In subsequent years, enthusiasm over the garden contest only became more intense: "The year of 1921 will long be remembered in the Elkhorn Division as most successful when considered from all angles. There were a greater number of gardens this year than ever before in the history of the division, and there were more vegetables grown than ever before." And the annual garden contest reached a new zenith of attendance: "At the conclusion of the season, large rallies were held in the Recreation Buildings at Burdine, Jenkins, Dunham and McRoberts, on August 23rd, 24th, 25th, 26th respectively. . . . So great an interest has been taken by all citizens in each community that the garden contest is now our greatest community gathering." So great was the interest in these rallies that the Recreation Buildings were able to hold only about two-thirds of the people who desired to attend. The contests could generate community spirit and even spark rivalries between towns. From Owings, West Virginia, came this notice in the *Mutual Monthly:*

> Once more our little town is out for the Garden Prizes. On all sides you can see our people working in their gardens. Much planting has already been done and many more seed beds are being prepared. Heretofore we have always won some of the prizes, but this time, we are after the Region Prize. We now serve notice on the rest of the mines, that they will sure have to go some if they beat the "Hill" this year. In about 30 days old "High Cost" will take a tumble at this place.

In much the same way that baseball rivalries, separate educational and religious facilities, and company-sponsored first aid contests sharpened the boundaries that distinguished one mining community from the next, the annual garden competition, whether by design or not, offered yet another opportunity for the company towns to compete against one another. Sociologist Sherry Cable, for one, has argued that barriers to communication and cooperation among mining communities were not effectively broken down until regional high schools were established in the 1960s.[39]

In the final analysis, the miner's garden presents us with some fascinating food for thought. While they undoubtedly improved the appearance of some towns—as the black-and-white prints plainly show—and made an important contribution to miners' kitchens, it has been argued that they represented yet another means through which some coal companies exerted control over their workers, for by encouraging families to raise their own food, management could justify paying lower wages. At least this is the argument that Paul Salstrom and Steve Hollenhorst make with respect to southern Appalachia:

> Southern Appalachia's backstage subsistence farming used to allow timber and coal industries to pay their workers low wages, at least until the United Mine Workers finally got a foothold in 1933. Prior

to that, Appalachia's coal companies often paid their workers below the cost of feeding and housing an average family. Most Southern Appalachian mine families, even in company-owned coal towns, raised vegetable gardens and also kept some livestock such as a cow, a pig, and a few chickens. In that way, Appalachia's widespread subsistence farming subsidized the region's early coal industry, keeping the market price of the region's coal low enough to compete against coal from states like Pennsylvania, Ohio, Indiana, and Illinois, where mines were much closer to the major coal markets. Southern Appalachia has been one of the leading U.S. examples of how the subsistence reproduction of workers can allow capitalists to pay workers less than a living wage.

On the other hand, gardens were valuable during periods of economic depression or low employment and when miners were called out on strike.[40]

Health Conditions

Although there are relatively few photographs depicting health conditions in the company towns, those that do exist help us to understand this important aspect of everyday life in the mining community. The most conspicuous pictures connected with this theme are of hospitals and visiting nurses (fig. 3.30). News of the comings and goings of the visiting nurses, statistics concerning number of visits made, and information pertaining to the crucial part they played in promoting and maintaining healthful conditions in the mining towns received a great deal of attention from the editors of the company magazine. This entry from 1921 described the job of the visiting nurse:

> The Consolidation Coal Company may truly be said to be pioneers in installing trained visiting nurses in mining towns, and in developing industrial visiting nursing service in the coal mining industry. The initial service, started in its Elkhorn Division, has been developed and extended until at the present time, 13 Visiting Nurses are employed on full time in the various divisions of our company. Visiting Nurses perform a multitude of duties, extending from bedside nursing in cases of emergency, to playground work with children. Included in the scope of their work are: domestic science classes, sewing classes, physical culture, first aid instruction, sani-

Fig. 3.30. "Community Nurse at Dunham. 10-6-21." Photographs of women are rare in the Smithsonian collection. Here a community nurse meets with a resident in Dunham, Kentucky.

tary inspections, directing Girl Scout troops, organizing and directing women's clubs; in fact general community work of every kind that tends to prevent disease, promote good health, inspire community interest, and create general usefulness.

According to company records, in the year 1920 visiting nurses made 29,045 total visits, including 11,209 nursing visits, 10,511 instructive visits, 7,288 social visits, and 37 school visits. Special attention was devoted to expectant mothers and prevention work. On the topic of prevention, the article states: "The having of trained nurses at hand has saved hundreds of lives during epidemics. With our company this was particularly true during the recent epidemics of Influenza."[41]

The reference to epidemics in the preceding paragraph is not insignificant. A survey of the *Mutual Monthly* attests to the fact that company town residents had to contend with a great variety of contagions—from influenza and measles to scarlet fever and typhoid to smallpox and diphtheria. Influenza was the most common malady. In March 1923 residents from Mine No. 29 in West Virginia reported that the influenza "epidemic is with us again, but we are glad to relate that it is not of a serious nature at this writing. It has hit us hard enough, however, to cut our working force considerably." From Mine No. 84 came this: "A great deal of sickness amounting to almost an epidemic is prevalent here. Most of the cases have been the La Grippe. The school attendance has been cut down nearly half, as a result." And from Mine No. 225 in Virginia: "'Flu' has raged in Seaboard for the past month; not one family escaped the prostrating disease. . . . There have been several deaths from this cause." It was not unusual for towns to impose quarantines on school children during particularly serious outbreaks.[42]

On a more positive note, the company's attempts to improve sanitary conditions in the coal towns did help to reduce the diffusion of diseases, as this report from Jenkins, Kentucky, affirms: "This community and the whole Division is ever striving to improve the existing excellent sanitary and health conditions. We have less smallpox, diphtheria, typhoid, flu and other preventable diseases here than in any other mining town within a radius of seventy-five miles." Another sure sign of improved health conditions in the mining town was the construction of a hospital equipped with state-of-the-art facilities. These buildings were often situated high on a hill, away from noise and dirt. Figure 3.31, showing a well-equipped doctor's office in Burdine, Kentucky, is also noteworthy for the poster on the far wall, which promotes mother's milk for newborns.[43]

Even a cursory glance at the photographs in this chapter conveys to the casual observer a sense of what life must have been like in one of Consolidation Coal's company towns during the first half of the twentieth century. The effectiveness of the images is enhanced substantially, however, when they are attended by captions or other notes and when they are situated in historical context. Images of black schoolchildren, immigrant miners sitting in an English class, and winners of garden competitions, for instance, take on greater meaning when we remind ourselves that segregation was alive and well in America during this period. Likewise, pictures of neat rows of houses are more meaningful when we realize they were designed, constructed, owned, and rented out by the company and thus were, in a very real sense, symbolic of the power of the big corporation.

Upon closer inspection, the photos reveal an array of "implicit"

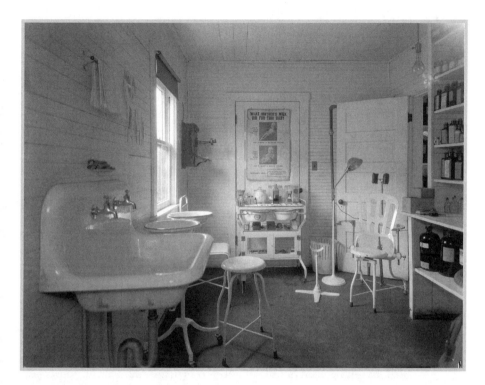

Fig. 3.31. "Doctors Office Burdine, Ky. 3-7-28."

landscapes. A central theme that emerges: standardization. This includes standardization of housing, town layout, and even the workforce. Such standardization was associated with a high degree of dependence on the part of labor. This includes dependence on the company for work, housing, education, food, manufactured goods, health care, and social services, manifested in the construction of houses, company stores, hospitals, schools, recreational facilities, and churches. The unmistakable result of standardization and dependence was effective control of the labor force. As Alan Banks concisely phrases it, "These company-controlled communities provided the infrastructural foundation for the maintenance and reproduction of new class realities in the mountains."[44]

While the images in the collection suggest a genuine effort on the part of the coal operator to meet the needs of workers, they also project an illusion of social progressiveness. The images of freshly whitewashed houses and churches, new recreation facilities and stores, not to mention the manicured gardens, indicate that Consolidation Coal—unlike some other coal companies—took pride in the appearance of its towns. As geographer Edward Relph notes, this is hardly surprising, given that one of the primary goals of such landscapes was to produce satisfied and productive workers. However, the photographs also advance the impression—a dubious one at best—that a "worker utopia" has been established in the mountains. In reference to company towns on Minnesota's iron ranges, landscape architect Arnold R. Alanen summarized the company strategy best when he concluded: "By adopting this approach, termed 'welfare capitalism' or 'social welfare,' mining company executives hypothesized that visiting nurses, recreational facilities, pension plans, and community beautification and sanitation projects would improve the efficiency of the work force and reduce the likelihood of strikes and labor disturbances." In the end, it was a desire to promote greater efficiency, productivity, and profitability that motivated company officials.[45]

Finally, the look of these towns expresses the Fordist managerial ethic of the time. As a "regime of accumulation," Fordism placed an emphasis on mass consumption and mass production. In the workplace, Fordism favored the increased application of corporate power, promoted detailed management and control of labor, and generally required that workers perform more routinized tasks. For management, this created a standardized and more economical situation to manage and control. In essence, each town came with its own interchangeable parts—workers, worker housing, company stores, and a managerial ethic. One has only to compare these landscapes with contemporary factory industrial landscapes to see the similarities. In this context, the landscapes of company towns are indicative of the vast changes sweeping through the American industrial economy during the late nineteenth and early twentieth centuries. In the landscapes of Consolidation's company towns, captured here on film, one can see such Fordist landscapes during their early, formative stages.[46]

Images of Work and Equipment

I have never seen a man who could do real work except under the stimulus of encouragement and enthusiasm and the approval of the people for whom he is working.

—Charles M. Schwab, 1928

"A Real Man's Work"

Anyone with ties to the coal-mining industry knows that underground mining is dangerous work. Although decades of technological innovations—from roof bolting to rock dusting and from improved ventilation to better mining equipment—have greatly improved conditions in the mines, coal mining remains a perilous occupation. For those of us who had come to believe that coal mining no longer posed serious risks to the underground worker, the near disaster at the Quecreek mine in 2002 caused us to amend our view. For four days in July, Americans focused their attention on Somerset, Pennsylvania, where a valiant rescue operation saved the lives of nine trapped miners.[1]

It must be conceded that coal mining has never been, nor is it likely to ever be, considered a glamorous occupation. Cutting and loading coal during the early years of the twentieth century was back-breaking work. It also could be dangerous. Even the most cautious and safety-conscious miner could be caught unawares in a dark and damp environment where poor ventilation, dust and gas accumulations, and roof falls were perils one confronted daily. If a miner emerged relatively unscathed after a long career working underground, years of inhaling coal dust could still end his life prematurely. Consolidation Coal was well aware of the profession's image problem. In 1923 the company addressed the issue head-on by informing anyone who would listen that coal mining was "a real man's work":

> How many mothers, who read this, desire their sons—the sons of coal miners—to become miners? We fear that the answer will be few, although when analyzed carefully why not? It is true coal mining is not a white collar occupation. It is not attractive to the molly-coddle, it is a real man's work. These facts eliminate the fastidious who will of course be more in place measuring ribbons behind some counter, or being supported by some good natured, hard working wife who still holds on to the job she had before marriage. The physically weak cannot stand up to the work. The man without nerve never makes a success underground, and many of those who are not thus eliminated, through choice or by circumstances or by conditions, have fond parents who would prefer their sons to be doctors, lawyers or ministers. And why not? There is nothing more natural than the deep interest parents have in their sons. The trouble is that parents and capable sons alike do not get the right slant on the vocation of coal mining. . . . Taken all in all, coal mining as a vocation affords comparatively steady employment, big pay, good working conditions and good living conditions, in addition to excellent and numerous opportunities for advancement. In fact, as compared with other vocations, coal mining is a desirable vocation which may lead to the realization of any competent man's highest ambition.

While living and working conditions may have been better in some of Consol's mining communities, it would be stretching the truth to say that conditions were good across the region. In some districts they were utterly appalling. As for "steady employment and big pay," by the early 1930s, even Consolidation Coal—a veritable giant in the industry—could no longer make that claim. And as historian Ronald Lewis has shown, the color of one's skin could place severe limitations on advancement.[2]

In chapter 3, we briefly explored the cultural diversity that was prevalent in mining communities across Appalachia and, more specifically, the ways in which this diversity was expressed on the landscape and in the photograph collection. Although tensions existed in the coalfields between whites, blacks, and recent immigrants from Europe, especially when blacks and immigrants were introduced to the coalfields as strikebreakers, historian Ronald Eller writes that a measure of harmony characterized relations between these groups, at least on the job:

> Social relationships with white miners were often ambiguous.
> Incidence of racial violence were not uncommon in the coal fields,
> especially during the early years, when lynchings and assaults were
> frequently reported in the local newspaper. The fact that many
> black workers were brought into the region as strike breakers did
> not ease the tensions. . . . Nevertheless, a relatively high degree of
> harmony existed between the races at a personal level. Working
> side by side in the mines, the men came to depend upon each other
> for their own safety, and the lack of major differences in housing,
> pay, and living conditions mitigated caste feelings and gave rise to a
> common consciousness of class.

If integration characterized relations in the mines, social interaction on the surface was a different matter. Here segregation and Jim Crow held sway for the black miner and his family. Writing of work in the mines during the 1940s, retired Consol miner Robert Armstead recalls:

> Though I had to accept segregation, it got to me. I had worked
> side-by-side in danger and coal dust with white fellows for nearly
> four years. Underground we were friendly, shared lunches and
> drinks, and helped each other. We came up out of the mine, said
> our friendly good-byes, and went our separate ways home to our
> families. Some said the black coal dust was a race equalizer. They
> said we were all black because of the coal dust, so blacks and whites
> blended, and there was less prejudice in a coal mine. I didn't really
> see it that way. Depending on each other to work safely and stay
> alive was a stronger bond down there than the mere presence of coal
> dust on a white man. . . . Above ground, attitudes were different.

Fig. 4.1. "Mine No. 9 Trip Ready for Dumping."

When those white fellows were out with their families or friends, they didn't know me. During my layoff I began to notice that many of those guys ignored me on the street. I had to change my thinking that they were my "mine buddies" and reduce them to my "former co-workers." That truth bothered me for a time, but I got over it.

Although not always subjected to the same sorts of overt discriminatory codes, foreign-born miners and their families also suffered from a variety of subtle—and not so subtle—forms of intolerance.[3]

Many of the "group" shots of miners show blacks and whites working or posing together. According to Lutz and Collins, pictures of people at work signal industriousness, a message Consol was surely interested in communicating to its workers via the company magazine. And as Jon M.

Fig. 4.2. "No. 205 Tipple Crew. 1921."

Williams and Daniel T. Muir point out, a group portrait "promotes a feeling of togetherness in any assemblage," yet another important idea the company was interested in sharing with its workers, for only through teamwork could more coal be loaded (fig. 4.1).[4]

Of course, not everyone associated with the coal industry actually worked in and around the mines, a point reflected in the content of the photograph collection. Also found are images of company salesmen, engineers, auditors, draftsmen, store clerks, machine shop crews, tipple crews, electric shop workers, as well as portraits of company officials—vice presidents, chairmen, treasurers, salesmen, and so on (figs. 4.2–4). Almost without exception, these individuals are men and they are white. Only very rarely do we come across photographs of women in the workplace. Exceptions include visiting nurses, switchboard operators at the telephone exchange, school teachers, and store clerks (figs. 4.5–6). Although small

Fig. 4.3. "Interior of Jenkins Bakery, November 6th, 1914."

Fig. 4.4. "Drafting Room, Office Building. Mar. 19, 1915."

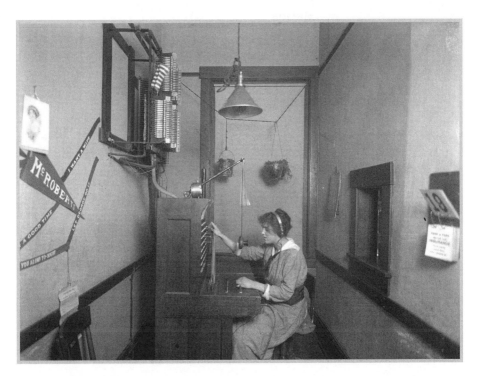

Fig. 4.5. "Telephone Exchange, March 19, 1915."

Fig. 4.6. "Dunham Store Clerks—4-6-28."

numbers of women likely worked in Appalachia's small "country bank" coal mines, their participation was often prohibited. According to Douglas L. Crowell, the virtual absence of women coal miners can probably be attributed to the superstition that a woman's presence in an underground coal mine was sure to bring bad luck. The bottom line here, as Richard V. Francaviglia firmly points out, is that "mining has traditionally been 'man's work,' and no amount of neutralized language can—or should—conceal that fact." Thus, it is safe to say that the vast majority of photographs that revolve around the work theme are of men working in the vicinity of the mine site.[5]

The miners depicted in this chapter did not have an easy life. Needless to say, only a miner employed by the company during this period could tell us exactly what it was like to work for Consolidation Coal in one of its underground mines, what risks miners faced, and what precautions they took. Fortunately, the Smithsonian photographs and other assorted historical data furnish us with a tantalizing window on the past.

Working in a Coal Mine

In 1898, William Jasper Nicolls gave us a glimpse—a virtual tour if you will—of a Consolidation Coal Company mine. Nicolls's brief underground "excursion" sets the stage for much of the rest of the chapter, for it was within confined spaces such as these that miners were subjected to the vagaries of their chosen line of work. Located in the Georges Creek valley of western Maryland, the Ocean No. 7 mine commenced operations in 1897 (fig. 4.7). According to Nicolls, one would be hard pressed to find a better example of drift mining than Consolidation Coal's Ocean No. 7:

> The entrance to this tunnel is arched with fine cut stone over an opening 12 feet in height and 17 feet 6 inches in width. Back of the arch the drift is lined with stone and brick masonry for a distance of 250 feet, up to the solid coal. If one is curious, and would penetrate farther into the bowels of the earth, the obliging superintendent will hand you a small miner's lamp,—a little teapot of oil with a flaring light which at first merely accentuates the Stygian blackness of the road. Soon, however, the tiny flame is reflected back and forth from the glittering walls of coal, and you can push forward with increasing confidence in your vision and your guide. It is not necessary to bend your head—like a duck walking under a bridge—as you

Fig. 4.7. "Mine No. 7 Portal." Notice the horse shoes hanging above the entrance to this western Maryland mine.

catch fleeting views of the dark, overhanging mass of roof. We are not in the thin, semi-bituminous seams of Pennsylvania. Here a man of full stature can walk upright and without fear of collision with the roof beams overhead, for the coal-seam is full 10 feet in thickness. At about half a mile underground, we come to the "face" or end of the tunnel. Here in a space about 10 feet wide and 9 feet high the miners are toiling with pick and bar, breaking down the coal; around us on every side is the black deposit of countless ages of time.

Of course, much has changed since the days when miners entered the workplace armed only with pick and shovel. Before the introduction of coal-cutting machines, continuous miners, and conveyors, however, the coal-mining industry relied primarily on human sweat and muscle to extract "black diamonds" from the earth.[6]

Initially, miners broke coal from the face using picks and wedges and then loaded it by hand into coal cars. Undercutting, drilling, and explosives—including gunpowder and dynamite—were used to loosen the coal, greatly increasing productivity in the mines. This was particularly important, as a miner's pay was directly linked to the amount of coal he mined. In an effort to boost productivity among the miners and, in the process, clear greater profits, the company trumpeted the accomplishments of its "champion" coal loaders via the pages of the *Mutual Magazine*. In one issue a photo of a black miner bears the caption, "Charles Smith . . . is the champion coal loader of Carolina. During the 24 working days of February, he loaded 875 tons of coal or an average of 36 11/24 tons per day. For the 24 days he drew down a pay of $385.00. Charles says the only reason he doesn't load more coal is because he can't get more wagons." From West Virginia came this report:

> Our mines have been running almost every day the past few weeks due to better car supply. This makes the miner smile for now he can show how much coal he can load. The champion coal loader at Mine No. 50 for the month of February, was George Baxter, who loaded 208 tons in 11 days, an average of almost 19 tons per day. The champion coal loader at Mine No. 94, was Houston Garner, who loaded 170 tons of coal in 10 days, an average of 17 tons per day. The champion coal loader at Mine No. 62, was Grover Collins, who loaded 204 tons of coal in 14 days, an average of almost 15 tons per day.

The notes from the Pocahontas–New River Division for the second half of 1924 are particularly noteworthy. In a section titled "Our Best Men," miners with the highest average daily earnings in the division were identified. Of the fifteen miners listed, five were identified as American, five Colored, two Hungarian, one Italian, one Slavish, and one Polish. By mentioning the ethnicity of the winners, the company may have been trying to convey to its diverse readership that hard work, regardless of who performed it, was good for business and would be rewarded accordingly. In addition to having their names printed in the company magazine, top cutters and car loaders also received prizes, but unlike the garden contests, no distinction appears to have been made between white and "colored" winners, reinforcing the notion that workers laboring underground were integrated but forced to adhere to a very different set of social practices on the surface.[7]

Fig. 4.8. "Miner loading car, Mine No. 26."

Especially popular during the First World War was the publishing of a barrage of slogans at the bottom of pages in the company journal to influence behavior in the mines: "Carelessness and Sorrow Travel Arm in Arm," "Make Safety Part of Your Every Day Work," "Through Co-operation All Things May Be Accomplished," "A Careless Man is Dangerous Not Only to Himself but to His Fellow Workers," "Loyalty and Skill Are Essential to Industrial Success," "The Bravest Man is One That Never Swerves from the Path of Duty," "Genius Counts for Less Than Diligence and Perseverance." And of course, coal loaders were constantly reminded to load "clean" coal. Thumbing through issues of *Consol News*, the company's magazine in the 1960s and 1970s, one is struck by how little things had changed in fifty years. Photographs of champion safety teams and miners with the fewest "lost-time" accidents, editorials connecting the importance of mining with America's position as a world power, and articles on company loyalty are everywhere in evidence.[8]

With demand for coal on the rise, the drive toward mechanization

gained momentum. One area where mechanization had a particularly pro-
found effect was in haulage. Back in the pick-and-hand-loading era, a
miner would have shoveled coal into wagons for transport to the surface
(fig. 4.8). Given that drift mines usually pierced the hillside at a slight
upward angle (to facilitate drainage) loaded cars could actually be rolled
out of the mine relatively easily. As miners tunneled deeper into the earth
and the distance to the surface increased, animal power replaced human
power as the principal means of haulage. Horses played an especially vital
role, as this note from the *Mutual Monthly* in 1926 certifies: "Allen Gains
recently made a trip to Enterprise to get two new horses for mine use.
When these are broken to work, they will greatly increase our output."
As mines grew and coal cars increased in size and tonnage, mechanical
and electrical haulage became increasingly necessary. By 1927 the company could even boast that it was operating the world's largest battery-
powered locomotive. Writing in the *Mutual Monthly*, company official
J. B. Hicks noted:

> Our company officials are constantly on the lookout for ways to
> make our mines safer for our men and increase efficiency so that
> our mines will be better places in which to work. In following up
> this policy the above photograph shows the largest main storage
> battery haulage locomotive in the world. It is of use especially in
> gaseous mines. Our company has nine of these locomotives in
> service. They haul 9,200 tons of coal daily. From time to time we
> are going to tell about some of the wonderful new mining machin-
> ery being developed by our company which has always been a pio-
> neer in new worth-while equipment.

As Hicks's last sentence intimates, mechanization's effects extended well
beyond the development of improved haulage equipment. Cutting machines, automatic loaders, continuous miners, conveyors, and numerous
other devices were on the horizon, if they were not already realities.[9]

According to promotional literature distributed by the company in
1989, the World War I years and the 1920s were marked by "incredible
prosperity." The coal industry "boomed—and Consol boomed with it."
During this interval, Consolidation Coal spent approximately "$3 million
annually on cutting and loading machines, faster underground transportation, and dramatically improved safety, working and living conditions for all Consol employees." As the succeeding paragraphs confirm,

mechanization was changing the coal industry in fundamental ways during this period. Whether the decade of the1920s could be described as one of "incredible prosperity" depends on one's perspective. We will examine this issue more thoroughly below.[10]

Katherine Harvey notes that Consolidation Coal played a leading role in the adoption of new technologies in the western Maryland coalfield. As early as 1905, for example, Consolidation was opening an electric plant near its Ocean No. 1 mine, "to provide light and power for that mine as well as a lighting system for Midland and other towns." In addition to aiding in illumination and ventilation, electric power was used to operate an impressive array of mining equipment. From Mine No. 26 in West Virginia, for example, came this report on the McKinley cutting and loading machine:

> New England mine is besieged with visitors from the coal fields all over the country, who come to see the McKinley cutting and loading machine operate. The machine cuts the coal and loads it in cars, drives a heading, leaving an arched roof, which makes timbering a back number. One man operates the machine. Recently a "Coal Age" representative was here, taking photographs of the machine and the coal it put out for market. He was loud in his praises of the machine. As this man sees them [coal cutters] all, his praise is very worthy of consideration.

In a speech before the American Mining Congress on 11 May 1928, H. F. McCullough outlined the advantages that shearing, cutting, and loading machines brought to the underground mines:

> In a field where narrow work mining is generally practiced, before the advent of the cutting machine five or six tons per miner and per place was a good performance. With undercut coal, the average increased to eleven or twelve tons per miner and per place. With sheared and undercut coal the average has been increased to from 18 to 25 tons per miner and per place. But with the latest types of cutting and shearing machines it is quite feasible to prepare from 40 to 50 tons per place in 6 ft. thick coal. With such tonnages available per place the application of loading machines becomes economically feasible and a farther degree of concentration is thereby made possible. . . . With the latest types of cutting, shearing and drilling

Fig. 4.9. "Arc Wall Mining Machine cutting coal 2-24-25."

machines it is frequently found that a crew will cut, shear and drill more tons of coal per shift than they formerly only undercut, and that they will use less effort and make higher wages than before.

McCullough also argued that such mechanization allowed for more easily loaded coal, minimized impurities, permitted a greater proportion of the largest sizes, reduced the cost of explosives, and lowered timbering costs. Reproduced in the pages of the *Mutual Monthly,* the article was accompanied by photographs of a Jeffrey Shearing machine (with drill), a Sullivan combination cutting and shearing machine (with drill), and a Sullivan shearing machine.[11]

Many of the images in the Smithsonian collection are of machinery and equipment, much of which was up to date and state of the art (figs. 4.9–10). No doubt these were taken primarily for insurance reasons. At the same time, one must bear in mind that company officials, in all likeli-

Fig. 4.10. "Joy Loading Machine Mine No. 206—12-6-26."

hood, took great satisfaction in the knowledge that the modern equipment the company had purchased was allowing its workers to remove more coal at a faster rate than many of its competitors. Thus the photographs of equipment were featured in middle management's photo albums. By 1926, Consolidation Coal's inventory included, among other things, 359 mine locomotives, 407 mining machines, 1,018 pumps, 223 power drills, 77 generators, 1,861 motors, 76 rotaries, 617 transformers, 132 fans, 159 boilers, 88 air compressors, and approximately 15,000 mine cars.[12]

Of course, the crews to which McCullough referred were getting smaller. While mechanization permitted greater amounts of coal to be removed, it had its drawbacks, at least from the perspective of the miner, for such technological innovations greatly reduced the need for a large

Fig. 4.11. "Future Coal Loaders of the Elkhorn Division." This image appeared in the *CCC Mutual Monthly Magazine,* May–June 1928.

labor force. The introduction of the automatic loader, for example, took a heavy toll on coal-loading jobs. According to Ronald Lewis, blacks felt the brunt of the new mining technology because they were disproportionately employed as hand loaders. One photograph found in the magazine but not in the Smithsonian collection shows nine naked black babies, some sitting, others standing. The caption reads "Future Coal Loaders of the Elkhorn Division," as if to underscore their limited employment opportunities (fig. 4.11). In reality, these children did not have a future with the company.[13]

Mechanization presented employers and employees with other problems as well. In mining's early days, miners walked to the coal face and relied on natural ventilation to disperse deadly mine gas and provide fresh air. As mines expanded in size, much time was lost walking to and from the mine face, and poor ventilation and illumination presented miners with serious health risks. In time, mechanical fans were employed to prevent the buildup of coal dust, methane, and blackdamp (a suffocating mixture of air and carbon dioxide or air and too much nitrogen). Candles—a dangerous source of ignition—were replaced by safety lamps and electrification. Similarly, the advent of trolleys and conveyors accelerated the removal of coal and facilitated the movement of miners from the mine entrance to the work site. While addressing some problems, these and other innovations created others. Now workers could be "crushed, run over, squeezed between cars, or electrocuted on contact with bare trolley wires." In addition, some new cutting machines produced tremendous amounts of coal dust—a key ingredient in mine explosions and the chief cause of black lung—and electrical equipment, including haulage equipment, generated sparks. As the next section endeavors to show, America's mine safety record during the first half of the twentieth century left much to be desired.[14]

Health and Safety

Coal mining, by its very nature, is a hazardous occupation. Today fatalities and serious injuries occur still, even under the best of conditions. During the nineteenth century and well into the twentieth, however, mine accidents were far more commonplace. Accidents associated with roof falls, ignition of mine gas and coal dust, the handling of mechanical haulage equipment, and, later, the operation of electric-powered equipment including improved illumination devices, trolleys, and conveyors, all contributed to a high accident rate in the U.S. relative to other coal-producing countries. As Corbin states, this was especially true of southern West Virginia:

> The miner who lived in southern West Virginia company towns worked in the most dangerous coal mines in the United States. Between 1890 and 1912 the mines of West Virginia had the highest death rate among the nation's coal-producing states; its mine-accident death rate was five times higher than that of any European country. Indeed, during World War I the southern West Virginia coal diggers had a higher proportional death rate than the American Expeditionary Force.

Economic growth, increased competition, and advanced technology have all been blamed for the high accident and fatality rates. Negligence on the part of miners in general and an inexperienced and poorly trained immigrant workforce, in particular, have also been offered as reasons for the poor record. For all their rhetoric, coal operators—bitterly opposed to unions and fearful of burdensome safety regulations—were responsible for standing in the way of meaningful safety reform.[15]

During this period, enactment of mine safety legislation rested primarily with the individual states. Pennsylvania, a pioneer in mine safety, passed the first substantive mine safety law in 1870. This act, which applied only to anthracite mines, called for coal operators to maintain accurate maps of workings, ensure the existence of at least two outlets at each mine, establish a minimum ventilation standard, and provide for the appointment of a competent mine boss as well as qualified mine inspectors. By the middle of the twentieth century, twenty-nine states had mine safety laws on the books. More often than not, these laws proved less than satisfactory and were poorly enforced. High fatality rates and persistent safety problems eventually kindled an interest in pursuing comprehensive federal legislation. Not until 1969, however, would such measures be enacted. Although the U.S. Bureau of Mines had been created in 1910—largely in response to a series of mine disasters—it was primarily an "information-gathering" agency. Remarkably, it was not granted the authority to inspect underground mines until 1941. Enforcement powers were not extended to the Bureau of Mines until 1953.[16]

Although statistics show that roof falls claimed far more lives, it was the ignition of methane gas and coal dust leading to mine explosions that struck fear in the miners and captured the attention of the nation. Areas where ventilation was poor and miners were employing candles or open-flame lamps for lighting and black powder to break up the coal face were especially susceptible to these sorts of accidents. After about 1880 safety in American bituminous mines deteriorated and the frequency of explosions rose sharply. Between 1891 and 1900 thirty-eight major explosions took place in American coal mines, resulting in 1,006 deaths. Clearly, a single accident in an underground mine could cause a horrifying number of deaths: 104 killed at the Fraterville mine in Tennessee in 1902; 112 killed in a Pennsylvania blast in 1902; another 179 fatalities at a Pennsylvania mine two years later; 169 lives lost at a Wyoming mine in 1903; 112 killed in a dust explosion in Virginia City, Alabama, in 1905; and two more explosions in Pennsylvania, one in 1907 and the other in 1908, resulted in 239 and 154 deaths, respectively.[17]

In terms of loss of life, however, none of these catastrophes could compare with the grisly disaster that took place at the no. 6 and 8 mines of the Fairmont Coal Company (which, by this time, had merged with Consol) in Monongah, West Virginia, on December 6, 1907. Of the 367 miners working underground at the time, only five made it out alive. According to historian Mark Aldrich, the company, which had merged with Consolidation Coal just two years earlier, connected the two mines to save the cost of sinking another shaft. Investigators later determined that ventilation at the working face had been poor and that open-flame lamps were being used despite the presence of dust and gas. The result was the worst mine explosion in American history. Just one year earlier, Andrew Roy, in *History of the Coal Miners,* had commented that "More

miners are annually killed by explosions in West Virginia, man for man
employed, or ton for ton mined, than in any coal producing State in the
Union or any nation in the world." The 1907 tragedy at Monongah only
affirmed what Roy and many others already knew—that America's
record of mine safety was shocking. Just thirteen days after the Monongah explosion, another blast—this one at the Darr Mine in Pennsylvania—killed 239 miners. Much needed to be done in the U.S. to address
this and other vital safety issues.[18]

How can we account for the frequency of explosions in U.S. mines
during this period? This was a question that weighed heavily on the minds
of those at the federal Bureau of Mines, whose mission it was to address
this problem. According to Aldrich, inspectors noted that mines were getting "deeper and gassier" and that miners often preferred to "shoot off
the solid" (blast without first undermining the coal)—a practice that
required the use of greater amounts of explosives. Aldrich also notes that
the rash of explosions took many coal operators by surprise, for many at
the time believed that coal dust alone could not set off an explosion, a
view that persisted into the 1930s in some quarters, even though European investigators as far back as 1803 were suggesting that it could.
Although the Bureau of Mines was hampered in its efforts by the fact that
its investigators could not enter mines without the permission of the coal
operators, its work eventually paid off. At the urging of the bureau, companies adopted new technologies that greatly reduced the risk. Given the
costs associated with the total destruction of a mine, it was certainly in the
best interest of the company to do what it could to minimize the risk of
future explosions. Safer mining machinery, first aid and mine rescue training, battery-operated cap lamps, improved ventilation, rock dusting (spray-
ing powdered limestone on mine roofs, bottoms, and ribs to neutralize the
explosive qualities of coal dust), and stricter enforcement of existing laws
combined to turn the tide. An upswing in fatalities from explosions during
the 1930s eventually prompted passage of legislation permitting federal
inspection of mines. By the late 1930s the explosion fatality rate started to
drop. And although the bureau was preoccupied with mine explosions,
roof fall accidents were also reduced thanks in large part to more effective
supervision, systematic timbering, and roof bolting.[19]

As early as the 1880s, Consolidation Coal had earned a reputation as
one of the safest mining companies. In 1895 the Maryland Bureau of
Industrial Statistics stated that "any miner in the region would resign his

Fig. 4.12. "Check board Mine 204—6-18-25."

present place were he assured of employment at the mines of this company. The mine superintendent is spoken of as fair, impartial, and considerate of the men's feelings, . . . [and] the mines are ventilated in the best method at present known." Historical evidence suggests that the company was addressing health and safety issues on a variety of fronts. In addition to erecting hospitals and, in some cases, providing on-site medical care and ambulances, the company instituted a "checking system" for keeping track of where men were at work in the mines. To go along with a photo of a "check board" from Mine No. 204 in Kentucky came this explanation: "The miner before entering the mine places his check on the line opposite the entry in which he works and under his room number. The board thus shows at a glance the location of every man in the mine, and should it be necessary to withdraw the men at any time it is an easy matter to get word to each man" (fig. 4.12). In some locations, the company also sponsored night school for miners. Among the subjects covered at one such school at the University of West Virginia at Morgantown were mine gases and their sources; ventilation; the use of the anemometer, water gauge, and barometer; methods of timbering, pumping, and drainage; and safety lamps and safety lamp testing.[20]

Like accidents, sickness resulted in lost time—something the company wished to minimize in order to maintain high levels of production. In the *Mutual Monthly* in 1921, Consolidation played up the health benefits of its new bathhouses:

> One of the greatest necessities, for health, as well as for the com-
> fort of the coal miner is the bath house, located at or conveniently
> near to the mine. . . . The temperature of the mines is uniform
> throughout the year, varying very little even during the coldest or
> hottest weather. During cold weather, the miner works in a tempera-
> ture which is much higher than the outside temperature. He leaves
> his work, wet with perspiration and upon leaving the mine,
> encounters the excessive cold. If there is a bath house near the
> opening, he goes directly there, washes up with a warm shower,
> changes to dry clothing and proceeds home in comfort, with no
> chance of taking cold, and the resulting lost time.

In a later issue, we are provided with another description of a new bath-house, while at the same time we are again reminded that the level of interaction between blacks and whites depended on whether or not one was working underground: "The colored section of the bath house is alike in practically every detail. The showers and tubs are located in the room into which the doors shown in the rear enter. Clothing is triced up to the ceiling where it hangs and drys [sic]. The chains used in tricing up the clothes are fitted with locks insuring the safety of the clothing" (see fig. 4.13). However, bathhouses and other such facilities were nothing new, as Harvey points out for western Maryland·

> By 1901 the Consolidation Coal Company had made some provi-
> sion for the comfort of men coming out of the mine, installing
> three bathrooms at the New Shaft for the use of employees who
> had to work all day in wet places in the Hoffman mine. A miner
> could "go to the Shaft in his Sunday clothes, take them off, take a
> check for them, hand his valuables to the keeper, put on his work-
> a-day suit, go down into the shaft, spend the day, come out, take a

Fig. 4.13. "No. 207 Washhouse—Interior. 5-8-21."

bath, put on his Sunday clothes, collect his valuables and reach home looking like the presiding elder." Meanwhile, his wet suit was placed in a dryer until the next morning.[21]

Consolidation Coal was also taking advantage of the Bureau of Mine's safety demonstrations. Photographs of first aid demonstrations, as well as of miners using equipment properly and improperly were taken and used as tools to convey the hazardous nature of mining work to new employees and to promote safety in the mines (figs. 4.14–18). Many Bureau of Mine safety demonstration pictures were distributed directly to managers and miners alike via the company's magazine, the *Mutual Monthly*. The photographs no doubt proved particularly valuable to recent immigrants whose facility with English was poor. According to William Graebner,

Native American [American-born whites] and older immigrant employees . . . complained of the safety hazards posed by those who

Fig. 4.14. "First Aid Meeting Jenkins, Ky. 4-29-16."

did not speak English. In response to these critiques, the safety movement after 1908 took on an educational hue. Universities in Illinois, Colorado, Kentucky, and other states offered institutes and short courses to train miners; the YMCA and the larger coal companies established night schools so that foreign miners could learn English. The Bureau of Mines used motion pictures to instruct miners who did not speak English.

According to Graebner, the jury is still out on whether immigrants contributed significantly to a high accident rate. Harvey, meanwhile, reported that the Georges Creek valley received its first visit from one of the bureau's "mine rescue and training cars" in 1910: "Much of the equipment demonstrated was intended primarily for gas and smoke victims and was not applicable to Georges Creek mining conditions. However, the demonstration of first aid for injuries from a fall of coal were particularly valuable, and the manager of the Consolidation Coal Company planned to organize a 'full-fledged corps of rescue men.'" As Graebner has pointed out,

Fig. 4.15. "THE WRONG WAY TO RIDE MOTOR."

Fig. 4.16. "THE RIGHT WAY TO RIDE MOTOR."

Fig. 4.17. "Accident caused by man getting caught with glove on brake lever."

Fig. 4.18. "Man getting killed between cars on curve 6-10-22."

coal operators were often reluctant to participate even in this, the simplest of safety steps. Mine safety problems were exacerbated by poor work habits on the part of some miners and an immigrant workforce sorely lacking in "elementary mining techniques" and ill-prepared to read safety materials and signs.[22]

Inspired perhaps by the Bureau of Mine's national first-aid meet in 1911 in Pittsburgh, Consolidation sought to encourage participation in safety and first aid training by holding annual contests at its mines (figs. 4.19–20). Held at the local baseball park or similar location, these events typically drew large crowds, such as this one in Pennsylvania:

> The sixth Annual First Aid Meet of Somerset County Miners was held on the Sipe Race Track field at Jenners [Jenner mine in Pennsylvania], Sunday, September the 8th. The attendance eclipsed that of all former events of its kind, fully three thousand people, representing every mining region in the county, witnessed the work of the competing First Aid Teams. In all 25 teams entered the contest for prizes offered by the management. Great interest in the work of the teams was manifested by the crowd which gathered on the hillside to watch the work of the teams and the judging by the physicians and visiting first aid men.

Prizes ranged from gold watches and cuff buttons to first aid certificates, fire extinguishers, nickel carbide caps, cap lamps, first aid charts, and instruction books. As this passage from 1921 hints, the mining community took pride in the effort of the local teams: "A large number of McRoberts people journeyed to Jenkins on May 14th, to see the First Aid contest between the teams of the Elkhorn Division; three of said teams being from McRoberts. We were proud of the work done by our teams, although they failed to secure first place."[23]

It was established earlier in the chapter that accidents have played an all too prominent role in American coal mining history. Even here the camera was put to use. In the event a miner was seriously injured or killed on the job, a photographer was summoned and the incident was captured on film (figs. 4.21–23). The "accidents" depicted in these images were usually reenactments of events that had taken place earlier. While they were probably used for insurance and legal purposes, the *Mutual Monthly* often published them along with "real-life" stories as a regular feature of its "Department of Safety" column. The stories of Tony Fadrovich, Horace E. Roberts, Gordon Hurd, and Lasco Papoish are illustrative. Fadrovich, a

Fig. 4.19. "First Aid Team, 1919."

Fig. 4.20. "Winning Team 1928—6-7-28."

Fig. 4.21. "Serious Accident to F.M. Tucker, McPeaks Branch—4-6-26."

Fig. 4.22. "Fatal Accident to Ralph Dandy—Mine No. 201—6-10-26."

Fig. 4.23. "Serious Accident to John Sestock, Mine No. 204—10-22-26."

coal inspector, was "picking slate from a trip [a string of coal cars] that was standing still on the tipple. He had his foot on the rail when the trip started to move," running over his foot. Roberts was less fortunate. He was "pushing loads back with the motor and had an empty car next to the motor. The empty car picked the switch [jumped the track] and wrecked. Motor bumpers were not protected with guards and the wrecked car slid up over the bumper, squeezing his leg between the end of the car and the controller. His thigh was broken, causing him to lose 124 days." Gordon Hurd was repairing a mine locomotive when a coworker "came over to the motor and pushed the trolley pole out of his way causing it to strike the wire and the motor to run forward mashing Hurd's leg against another motor." Lasco Papoish's story is the most tragic of the four. He was "pushing a car to the dump and walking back of same. Several cars broke loose and followed after him, catching him between the bumpers and throwing him on his knees. He was dragged between the cars until the front car struck the car on the dump. His legs were crushed causing injuries from which he died." Two important messages were being broadcast: that carelessness leads to serious injury or death and that lost time hurts the company. What more graphic way for the company to drive these points home than through photographs?[24]

The "Department of Safety," a regular column of the *Mutual Monthly,* also published tips on the proper operation of equipment and what to do in the event of an accident. In one issue, special emphasis was placed on the practice of exposing hands underneath moving motors. Several stories were recounted where miners had their fingers cut off by the wheels of a moving motor, some of which were accompanied by photographs. A "Department of Safety" column from October 1918 stressed the importance of the magazine's "Safety Bulletin Boards":

> Are you receiving the benefit you should from reading and discussing the Safety Bulletins sent out every two weeks and posted at your mine? Are these bulletins reaching out to you and helping you be more careful? These bulletins do not portray a highly improbable condition that exists principally in the imagination but they show conditions that do exist and cause accidents in American mines. In the mines of our own Company accidents closely paralleling these bulletins are to be found each year. Going back but a short way will give enough examples to convince you that it is well to read them and to realize that an accident of the same kind may happen to you if you take a like kind of chance.

While a 1922 column declared that the company's safety department resolved "that each and every employe of this company would be given an opportunity to learn first aid if he desired to do so" and that "nearly one thousand of our employes did take advantage of these night schools during the previous year," another column boasted that a worthwhile record had been set at the mines of the Maryland Division. Over the course of three and a half years, "800 Men Worked 43 Months" and "Produced 2,200,000 Tons of Coal Without a Fatal Accident." According to the magazine, this accomplishment was "not due to naturally good conditions but to overcoming what is classed as the most dangerous and treacherous [*sic*] roof in any mines we operate. . . . these naturally dangerous mines have been made over into the safest mines of any we operate. With equal effort upon your part, your mine can have as good a record."[25]

While there may have been genuine interest on the part of the company to promote safety in the mines—it was certainly in their best interest to do so—it must be remembered that much of this effort was initiated after the Monongah disaster. Seen in this light, it is possible that the health and safety photographs were also utilized to restore the reputation of the company in the eyes of employees, government mine inspectors, and the general public, and to forestall efforts to impose stringent safety legislation.

Union Activity

When we think of the history of coal mining in Appalachia during the first half of the twentieth century, we naturally think of the "wars" that were fought in every mining district when the union organizers came to town—bitter, sometimes violent struggles that pitted management against labor and, often, miner against miner. We think of the Paint Creek–Cabin Creek strike, Blair Mountain and Matewan, of Baldwin-Felts guards and Mother Jones. However, with the exception of one small album showing miners and their families marching and picketing in the Fairmont region of West Virginia in 1932 and one powerful photograph of a bloodied miner being restrained by two police officers, evidence of union activity and of violence is largely omitted from the Consol photograph collection (figs. 4.24–26). Given the fact that most coal companies were vehemently opposed to unions of any kind, it should come as no surprise that few photographs in the Smithsonian collection focused on this theme. While the number of photographs showing union activity are relatively few, the effect that unions had on the industry cannot be overstated. Nor can it be ignored.[26]

By the early years of the twentieth century, coal companies had come to dominate life and labor across large parts of Appalachia. Dealing from a position of power, coal operators used any and all means to resist the unions. The key was to use subtle and, on occasion, not-so-subtle means to ensure that workers understood that what was good for the company was good for the country—that they equated loyalty and hard work with a prosperous America. Workers—even school children—were told in no uncertain terms that America had many enemies. Some, like the Kaiser,

Fig. 4.24. Disputes between management and labor and between union and non-union miners sometimes turned violent, as this image from a 1932 Fairmont strike album shows.

Fig. 4.25. The presence of women on the picket line is suggestive of the role they played during strikes.

Fig. 4.26. In this photograph, taken from the 1932 Fairmont strike album, it is readily apparent that a measure of cooperation among different ethnic groups characterized life on the picket line.

or simply "the Hun," were bold enough to present themselves in broad daylight. Others—Bolsheviks, communists, anarchists, socialists, and other "radicals"—lurked in the shadows. They were even more dangerous, for they poisoned the hearts and minds of unsuspecting men. According to the coal operators and organizations such as the American Constitutional Association, the only way to combat these forces and preserve America's freedoms was to stand shoulder to shoulder, resist the overtures of the union organizers, and work diligently for the company. As one might expect, this message was trumpeted loudly in the pages of the company magazine, as well as through other outlets. This editorial from March 1923 presented the situation in black-and-white terms:

> Disloyal propaganda is the real cause of the major portion of labor's unrest. The agitator tells the workman he can by revolt acquire what he wants without work. . . . Whither go we? Wherever we ourselves elect. Wherever we as citizens of the greatest country on earth decide we will go. We can remain firmly on the safe road of conservatism that leads to peace and prosperity, or

we can plunge over the cliff to total destruction by permitting our enemies to take the helm. Loyalty to country, loyalty to industry, honest toil, economy in all things and co-operative effort between all factors of industry will save the day for America.

One laconic editorial from 1922 put it even more simply: "And to those who would destroy the very foundations of our government, it must be made plain that Americans stand for law and order and against anarchy and destruction." This proved a particularly powerful message to recent immigrants, who were no doubt eager to show they were not foreign agitators but rather "good Americans."[27]

In the case of Consolidation Coal, strict adherence to the tenets of Taylorism, with its emphasis on efficient organization and control, as well as welfare capitalism and industrial Americanization was critical if the unions were to be defeated. Early on, proponents of welfare capitalism recognized that "company flexibility and benevolence" could have a positive effect on production and, more important, could effectively stave off the advances of the unions. In addition, welfare capitalism could enhance company control over workers, both in the workplace and at home. The idea was to satisfy the needs of workers to the extent that they would not feel compelled to join a union. If this did not work, a variety of other means could be employed to coerce and intimidate workers, maintain law and order, and promote stability. Industrial Americanization, on the other hand, was a strategy championed by "a class-conscious minority of socially, politically, and professionally well-positioned leaders" that favored a "hierarchical vision of community and nation"—one in which "free-market business principles" were wed to "national loyalty" in an attempt to ensure a "literate, loyal, and obedient producing class." One of the goals of Americanization, therefore, was to instill in recent immigrants the notion that "loyalty to the state and nation" was "interchangeable with obedience to one's employer, teacher, or leader." The message to workers was simple—management and other elites knew what was best for the working class and, therefore, "were justly empowered to control the work and social experiences of others." What was good for the company was good for the worker.[28]

According to John C. Hennen, one of the key components of Americanization was the "American plan." Hennen notes that the CCC *Mutual Monthly* was "an aggressive promoter" of the American plan, the ultimate goal of which was to paint unions as dictatorial, greedy, and un-American. At the same time, company officials wanted employees to associate the open shop with greater freedom. Thus the purpose of the American plan was to expose the unions for what they were, or at least what the company owners wanted their workers to believe they were:

> By an American plan is meant one wherein the worker has a decisive voice in matters pertaining to his work and is not dominated by foreign agitators who are not posted as to local conditions and not interested except in their own affairs. In brief, an American Plan is one of freedom, personal freedom, of the worker to carry out his own wishes as relates to his work, and is so called because the word "American," as applied, means freedom from tyranny—freedom to act—freedom from the burden of picking the other fellow's chestnuts from the fire and the accompanying burnt fingers and no profit. Freedom from the distress and suffering accompanying strikes called for the benefit of others and for the purpose of advancing the personal causes of agitators who live by stirring up strife in order that their services may be needed to quell the disturbance.[29]

Coal operators safeguarded their interests in a variety of other ways as well. The Fairmont Coal Club serves as a case in point. Organized "to promote harmony" among operators in the northern West Virginia coalfields, the club met weekly to exchange ideas. Aretas Fleming Jr.'s involvement in the group is particularly noteworthy:

> A. Brooks Fleming, Jr., production manager of the northern West Virginia section of the Fuel Administration, was active in the formation of the club. Fleming was a director of the Consolidation Coal Company and an assistant to the company's president. Son of the eighth governor of West Virginia, Fleming also served as a director of the Northern West Virginia Coal Operators Association, the Fairmont Land and Building Corporation, the National Bank of Fairmont, and many other corporate enterprises. As fuel administrator, Fleming's duty was to forward information and recommendations on coal production to the U.S. fuel administrator in Washington.

Fleming's myriad interests led to charges of conflict of interest. That these charges were never taken seriously is illustrative of the power of the coal industry and the degree to which such influence peddling guided government policy during this period.[30]

World War I presented companies with a new set of challenges.

Responding to pressure from the Wilson administration to increase wartime production, operators entered into what they saw as a temporary agreement with the unions, one that prohibited the coal companies from firing miners if they joined a union. In the years after the war, federal support for the unions waned and the operators retrenched. Citing the U.S. Supreme Court's decision in the 1917 case *Hitchman Coal and Coke v. Mitchell,* in which yellow-dog contracts (forbidding union membership) were ruled legal, coal operators set out to reclaim ground lost to the unions.[31]

In a speech to the Newcomen Society of America in 1955, George Love noted that in July 1925, Consolidation Coal announced its intention to "operate non-union." By the 1930s, however, the advantage had shifted once again in favor of the unions. Passage of the National Industrial Recovery Act (1933), the bituminous coal code, or "Appalachian Agreement" (1933), the National Labor Relations, or "Wagner," Act (1935), and the first and second Bituminous Coal Conservation, or "Guffey," Acts (1936 and 1937) signaled a sea change in management-labor relations. Among other things, these pieces of New Deal legislation paved the way for an eight-hour work day, a forty-hour work week, higher wages, and collective bargaining. A minimum work age of seventeen was established. Any requirement that employees patronize only the company store, use only company scrip, or rent only a company house was struck down. The victory was a hollow one in many respects, however. Although personal liberties were secured and vital labor issues addressed, some scholars, including Paul Salstrom and Jerry Bruce Thomas, have argued that the higher labor costs associated with these advances ended up raising prices and accelerating the drive toward mechanization. Thus the benefits were passed on to an increasingly smaller labor pool.[32]

The Economic Picture in the 1920s

Earlier in this chapter reference was made to recent promotional literature circulated by the company that alluded to the company's "incredible prosperity" during the 1920s. Although not readily apparent in the photographs, evidence gleaned from the company magazine suggests that many of the company's mines were experiencing hard times during that decade. Numerous scholars have shown that the coal industry in general and miners in particular were feeling the tremors of the Great Depression well before the stock market crash of 1929. Historian Jerry Bruce Thomas captures the tenor of the times:

> In truth, coal in the twenties provided the classic case of an industry beset with overcapacity and its associated ills: market gluts, chronic losses, frequent bankruptcies, and low wages. The industry expanded beyond the capacity of its markets not only because of the demand generated by World War I but also because railroads offered low rates to encourage the buildup of coal traffic. West Virginia . . . competed with producers nearer to industrial markets by maintaining nonunion operations, and in the case of the Pocahontas and New River fields, by shipping a high grade of low-sulphur coal favored by the metallurgical industries. The success of West Virginia operators in defeating postwar organizing efforts of the United Mine Workers of America (UMWA) encouraged the opening of new mines. Then demand shrank as natural gas, petroleum, and electricity ate into coal markets; new inventions permitted more economical use of coal; and consuming industries grew more slowly. Under these circumstances it became difficult to sell coal at a price that covered costs of production. Operators, faced with substantial fixed costs, sought to avoid bankruptcy by reducing wages or by using labor-saving machinery. Miners, their families, the coal mining communities, and West Virginia suffered the consequences.

The economic tailspin devastated many families: "As the Depression deepened in West Virginia, it produced conditions that were among the worst in the country. Coal production fell from 146 million tons in 1927 to 83.3 million in 1932, and some thirty-three thousand coal industry jobs disappeared, leaving many coal miners trapped in futility and hopelessness." As if losing one's job was not bad enough, miners and their families also had to contend with evictions, malnourishment, and disease. Many had nowhere to go. Stranded in isolated coal camps and unable to leave without outside help, most of the unemployed probably knew they could not return to mining. However, they were unprepared for any other line of work. This sort of despair does not make its way into the CCC images. Even a company with the financial resources of Consolidation Coal was vulnerable to the economic upheavals of the 1920s and 1930s.[33]

Notes submitted to the *Mutual Monthly* from the mining communities serve as powerful testimony that Consolidation Coal was feeling the effects of a situation in which there were too many mines and too many miners. Warning signs started to emerge as early as 1921, as this entry from Idamay, West Virginia, indicates: "Although work was somewhat slack for a month or so, very few of our men left. They are 'standing by the ship,' realizing no doubt that conditions are not better elsewhere and that to move around means loss of time and money. The living and working conditions of Idamay are so far superior to other mining communities that a little slack work does not discourage our men." At some mines, the stretches of "slack" time dragged on for months before work resumed, much to the relief, no doubt, of the miners and their families. Mines Nos. 50, 62, and 94 in West Virginia, for example, reported a fourteen-month shutdown, before work resumed in November 1922. At Mine No. 13 in Maryland in 1922, the outlook was hopeful: "Our coal production has not been very great at this mine lately, but we hope to improve it considerably in the near future if circumstances permit." Four months later, in March 1923, the news was indeed good: "All our mines in this division are enjoying a rather unusual condition which is fully appreciated by our men. We have a full railroad car supply and are working six days a week." By January 1923, Mine No. 27 could submit a positive report to the magazine: "Mine No. 27, which has been closed down since July 30, 1921, has resumed operation again with all the old employees back on the job. Many of them had gone to other places to work but returned as soon as the mine started here. This speaks well for our Superintendent, Mr. Swisher, as it shows the men are all satisfied and want to remain on the job." The mood was cautiously upbeat in Kentucky during this interval as well. In January 1923, Mines No. 206 and No. 207 reported:

> Because of the car shortage during the past two months the town of Dunham has seen a number of its residents depart for other fields. This has depressed so much that we haven't had anything encouraging to say about ourselves. However, conditions are looking up and old faces are reappearing. We breathe a sigh of relief and take a new grasp on our community interests and take an optimistic view for the remaining winter months.

Things could—and would—get much worse in succeeding years. By 1925 the mining "slump" had settled in for a long stay. The resulting hard times are revealed in a terse yet heartrending statement drawn from the *Mutual Monthly* in 1925:

The mine worker who has steady work these days is a man to be envied, and all such should appreciate their good fortune. Thousands of miners have been idle for months, hoards of others have been working an average of about two days per week, just enough to keep body and soul together. On the other hand many mines have been working full time at a good living wage and their workers are prosperous.[34]

The company's response to the economic downturn was to remind its workers of how good they really had it. In its Thanksgiving Day 1921 message, the editors of the *Mutual Monthly* did not mince words:

At first thought, without delving into real conditions and without comparing our lot with that of other peoples of the world, many of us may not feel that we have much to give thanks for this year. Business is bad, work is slack, prices are high, and things look generally blue—to many of us. But let us look behind the screen. Let us make comparisons, not with the boom times of the war, but let us go back a bit farther, to 1914 for instance. Stop here—and recall just how you were fixed then. Did you have that automobile you now use? Did you wear silk shirts in 1914? Did you own those liberty bonds and did you have that bank account? Many of us must answer "No" to one or more of these and similar questions that could be justly asked.

A similar note was struck at the end of 1922 in an editorial ominously titled "The Dying Year": "Another year, eventful in the coal industry, is about to pass into history, a year filled with tragic happenings, industrial strife, suffering and sorrow, and yet with it all there is much for which we should be thankful, for through the lessons taught, through experiences we have had, through the hardships we have suffered, we should be better fitted to handle like situations should they present themselves in the future." In accounting for the crisis, Consol officials were quick to point out that large operators, who provided modern facilities for their mining population and state-of-the-art machinery for their mines, incurred higher production costs than small operators, who provided no amenities. Officials also conceded that the industry had probably overdeveloped as a result of increased wartime demand. Now a lull in demand from the transportation sector and the steel industry was taking a mighty toll on the coal industry: "Today there are thousands of idle cars, and motive power a plenty, but the steel mills and other big industries are running only part time and the demand for coal is light, in fact so light that comparatively speaking we may truthfully say there is no demand for bituminous coal." And of course the company was always willing to place a fair share of blame for economic troubles on the unions.[35]

Perhaps the most obvious sign that all was not well with the coal industry could be found on the back cover of the May–June 1928 issue of the *Mutual Monthly:* "Till we meet again. We regret to announce to our employees that on account of the present conditions within the coal industry, we have decided to discontinue the publication of the Mutual Magazine. This issue will be the last."

Images of Environmental Transformation

A crystal torrent, a mud stained funnel,
Where the water pours out of the great mine-tunnel,
Emptying its saffron and sulphur-stained stream
In the cups of the valleys of mist and dream.

—Bentztown Bard, "Frostburg," 1918

The opening up of the coal deposites [*sic*] in the region and the high rate of wages for all kinds of labor, is attracting to this section a large and industrious population. . . . 'Tis rather sad to think that our magnificent pine forests are disappearing so rapidly. With three steam saw mills in constant operation, cutting 15,000 feet of lumber daily, we will soon have nothing but vast fields of ugly stumps.

—*Cumberland (Md.) Union and Allegany County Gazette, 1865*

Photography and Environmental Alteration

There are two things we can almost always count on when it comes to mining. First, we end up removing more material than we actually need. To get to the precious metal or the fuel mineral we desire, we must first excavate that which stands in the way. Thus we strip away vegetation and topsoil, sink shafts and dig tunnels, gouge massive open pits into the earth, and even blast the tops off mountains. The end result is a mining landscape made up largely of additive and subtractive features like gob piles (slate dumps) and open pits. This brings us to the second point—satisfying our voracious appetite for mineral resources carries with it a hefty environmental price tag. Nowhere is this more evident than with our historic coal-mining landscapes. Decades after operations have ceased, the railroad tracks have been pulled up, and the company town has been abandoned or dismantled, the imprint of mining—that "symbolic antithesis of agriculture"—still remains on the land, a testament, if ever there was one, to our ability to alter and reshape the physical land-scape.[1]

With extensive coal and timber holdings in several states, as well as loading, shipping, and sales facilities in a handful of others, Consolidation Coal possessed the capacity to alter Appalachia's physical environment on a truly grand scale. Thanks to narrow-gauge logging railroads, steam-powered sawmills and earth-moving equipment, and an assortment of other technological innovations—pumps, vents, drills, coal-cutting machines, and automatic loaders, to name but a few—a valley in western Pennsylvania, southern West Virginia, or eastern Kentucky could be transformed beyond recognition almost overnight. In relatively short order, silent forests and small agricultural fields could be supplanted by rows of company houses and miles of railroad track. With the commencement of mining operations, it would not take long for local streams to succumb to the effects of the acid backwash pumped from the mines or from the contaminated water emanating from the ever-growing number of waste piles.

The photographs featured in this chapter tell the story of environmental transformation that took place on company-controlled land prior to the Second World War. That Consolidation Coal recorded the environmental devastation on film comes as a surprise to many of us today. At first glance the pictures appear to provide the sort of damaging evidence—the smoking gun, if you will—that would have cast the company's mining practices in the worst possible light. In present-day parlance, they would have presented the company with a "public relations nightmare." At least that is how a spectator firmly situated in the early twenty-first century might be tempted to read them. But that is not how the photos were viewed at the time they were taken. Therefore we must ask, Why were they taken and for whom?

One could argue that these photographs—perhaps even more than the others—need to be considered in historical context. As historians Brian Black and David Nye have ably shown, what we might regard today as wanton environmental destruction was likely perceived very differently by a majority of Americans in the early years of the twentieth century. Black, for instance, describes the despoiled landscapes of western Pennsylvania's oil boom:

> The views of Petrolia were unlike any scene witnessed previously, and yet few observers felt alarm or hesitation when confronted with them. Even when the ethics and techniques of the industry

caused repeated fires and floods, the oil industry and its boom were seen almost exclusively in an emphatically positive light.

Much as natural wonders were depicted in art and literature as "sublime," the American trust in progress allowed sites of industry not to remain unsightly views of dirt and grime, but to become wonderful visions of the future through the idea of the "technological sublime." The idea of the technological sublime made industrial change an ideal and therefore increased its ready acceptance.

Much the same can be said of coal-mining landscapes. As the excerpt from the poem at the beginning of this chapter clearly shows, the environmental transformation that inevitably went hand in hand with mining even served as a source of romantic inspiration to some.[2]

Black's comments are reminiscent of Susan Sontag's remarks regarding the unexpected beauty one is liable to encounter if given the opportunity to peer through the viewfinder of a camera: "In principle, photography executes the Surrealist mandate to adopt an uncompromisingly egalitarian attitude to subject matter. . . . Black factory buildings and billboard-cluttered avenues look as beautiful, through the camera's eye, as churches and pastoral landscapes. More beautiful by modern tastes." Anyone who has ever admired an Edward Hopper painting of rooftops and water towers in New York City, a David Plowden photograph of rail yards and grain storage bins, a Clarence Carter painting of a steel mill, or an album of Farm Security Administration prints has no doubt experienced this sensation.[3]

Even if we do not find a painting or photograph aesthetically pleasing, an image may still evoke a positive response from the viewer. In the foreword to Stanley Greenberg's recent book *Invisible New York: The Hidden Infrastructure of the City,* Thomas H. Garver points out that many large nineteenth-century factories were made up of "closely built, multistory, solid brick structures surmounted by the belching smokestacks of the power plant." Contrary to what we may believe today, in the eyes of the coal industry and perhaps Americans in general during the 1920s and 1930s, "Smoke," in Garver's words, "meant business, and pollution meant progress." While the smokestacks may have held very little in the way of visual appeal, to many Americans at the time they may have been a source of pride. As Black has argued, photographs of industrial scenes may have served another important purpose: "The effort to take a site of industry and not simply accept it, but instead to celebrate and revere it as an icon of progress, is a product of the technological sublime in nineteenth-century society. The photographic record enhanced this by making residents and users less afraid of massive changes." Considering the scale of the changes taking place at this time, the point is an important one. Taken together, these ideas may explain the primacy of the environmental alteration photographs in the Smithsonian collection and, further, why Consolidation Coal was not compelled to screen such images to safeguard its reputation. Not only did the photographs of environmental alteration allow the company to record the development of a mine site over time, they also could be used to show how the company was winning black diamonds from the earth which, in turn, was propelling the nation to industrial greatness. It is highly unlikely that most Americans today would interpret the images in the same way.[4]

Following this line of thought, geographer Mary-Louise Quinn, whose research has focused on the Appalachian Copper Basin in Tennessee—notes that postcards were printed showing the Ducktown Sulphur, Copper and Iron Company's sulfuric acid plant in Isabella. Postcards were also printed of the Tennessee Copper Company's early sulfuric acid plants. In Quinn's opinion, the printing of postcards is "a strong indication that the structures were a source of real pride" to the companies. This seems to be the case with Consolidation Coal for the company printed postcards of some of its coal mines—suggesting a similar pride in its operations (fig. 5.1).[5]

Geographer Homer Aschmann describes four distinct stages of development through which a mine inevitably passes. During the first stage, *prospecting and exploration,* surveyors and geologists examine the proposed mine site to determine whether or not it is in the company's best interests to acquire the mineral rights and undertake the mining process. In the second stage, *investment and development,* the company establishes the infrastructure necessary to remove the minerals in a cost-effective manner and ship them to market. Given the initial capital investment, high-grade "bonanza" deposits are mined first to ensure an early return to investors. Technological advancements allow lower grade ores to be mined during the third stage, the period of *stable operation.* Finally, in the fourth stage, the mine enters a period of *decline* when either the vein has been entirely exhausted or, as is more often the case, when the cost of production rises too high. One aspect of mining that Aschmann fails to touch on is that each of the stages in the sequence is accompanied by environmental modification of some kind. Nevertheless, Aschmann's four-

Fig. 5.1. "Consolidation Coal Co's Mine 'Ocean No. 7' near Lonaconing, Md." That this photograph was colorized and used as a postcard suggests that such images were viewed in a very positive light during the early years of the twentieth century. Courtesy Frostburg Museum, Frostburg, Maryland.

stage framework is useful to retain as a guide when inspecting the photographs that follow. As Marion Clawson reminded us in 1972, private landowners during the nineteenth century in particular—and we must, of course, include coal mine operators among them—often exercised little restraint when it came to considering the potential impacts their actions had on the physical environment. As we shall soon see, in practice the first decades of the twentieth century were no different. As the photographs in this chapter demonstrate, alteration of the physical environment took on many forms and occurred during each of Aschmann's four stages of mine development. In addition to the geomorphological changes one usually associates with mining activities—the gob piles, tunnels, and open pits—there were impacts to timber and water resources as well.[6]

Reshaping the Land

The best way to examine the photographs in this section is in chronological order. Only in this way can we come to appreciate fully the complete transformation that took place over time throughout Appalachia's coal lands. This format is all the more effective when one takes into account that there are pictures representing nearly every aspect of mine development and operation, from exploration and surveying to logging and site preparation and from mine excavation and town construction to water pollution and waste disposal (fig. 5.2).

Before a coal company could even think about developing the mineral resources of an area, it first had to secure rights to the mineral resources and then establish a reliable transportation link between the future point of production and the intended point of consumption. With regard to the former, Jack Weller writes,

> As coal became a necessary fuel, men of industry again came to the southern mountains, this time to bargain for the coal deposits. Land companies were formed, and their representatives bought up vast tracts. Again the mountaineer found himself at a disadvantage. Often he did not know that there was coal in the land he owned or had no knowledge of its extent. . . . The mountaineer would sign contracts he could not read, even bargaining away the rights to the land he wanted to keep for his farm and family. Only in later years was he to discover that he had hardly a scrap of right left to his homestead place.

While such dubious transfers no doubt took place—the infamous broad-form deed alluded to above was surely the most deplorable legal means by which mountaineers were hoodwinked into signing away their property rights—recent scholarship has shown that some local residents actually expedited the process on behalf of the coal companies. Often these individuals were themselves speculators who accumulated property rights and later sold them to coal companies. In other cases, they were hired by coal companies to acquire land and manage their properties. Either way, they facilitated and accelerated the process by which the rights to coal resources were transferred from local residents' hands to outside corporate hands. As Harry Caudill, Ronald Eller, John Gaventa, and numerous others have shown, these corporate entities were generally owned by absentees. Firmly ensconced in office buildings in New York, Baltimore, or elsewhere, owners and key officials were rarely on hand to witness the environmental consequences of the coal industry's actions.[7]

Some of the most powerful images in this section are not of denuded hillsides or polluted streams. Rather, they are of forested hillsides and fields of corn—some of which are planted on extremely steep slopes— enclosed by worm, or zigzag, fences. At first glance, it appears as though

Fig. 5.2. "Garbage Disposal Dump McRoberts, Ky." It would be difficult to imagine a coal company today recording its waste disposal practices in this way.

we are looking at nothing more than scenes from a mountaineer's farm. To truly grasp what these photographs are disclosing, however, we must turn to the captions, for these images are, in reality, coal-mining landscapes in the making. In effect, the company is presenting us with images of the land as it looked on the eve of industrialization. Figure 5.3, for instance, is showing us more than just a wooded hollow; it is spotlighting the future location of the power house at Mine No. 202. Similarly, figures 5.4–6 are not merely black-and-white prints of a mountain farm in eastern Kentucky; they show places that are on the verge of being obliterated to make way for workers' houses, a tipple, and a tramway. Soon, the trees will be cut and the corn will wither as the hillside is sliced away to expose the coal seam (figs. 5.7, 5.8). Then the coal will be faced for opening and tunnel excavation and mine construction will begin in earnest (fig. 5.9).

The swiftness with which these changes were brought about was indeed impressive, as the following passage from the July 1918 issue of the *Mutual Monthly* succinctly relates:

Fig. 5.3. "Power House location, No. 202 Mine, September 8th, 1911."

Fig. 5.4. "Location for Houses No. 206 Mine, Sept. 16, 1911."

Fig. 5.5. "Tipple location No. 203 Mine, September 8th, 1911."

Fig. 5.6. "Tramway location No. 203 Mine, September 8th, 1911."

Fig. 5.7. "No. 203 Mine Opening, Sept. 24, 1911."

Fig. 5.8. "Coal faced for opening No. 203 Mine, Oct. 2nd, 1911." The first stage of tunnel construction is underway.

Jenkins [Kentucky], and its "Five Thousand," its many and varied structures fashioned of wood, stone, steel, brick and concrete, is becoming more modern every day with its improved streets and pretty green parks. No wonder it is frequently alluded to as "the most wonderful mining town in the country." It seems strange to speak of it as being only seven years old, when, in fact, the place itself and the "Elkhorn Coal that has already made it famous have been here 'always.'"

The article goes on to identify one of the area's early residents, John W. Wright. As Wright and others like him across Appalachia sold their land, Consolidation Coal amassed the mineral riches that would one day enable it to develop into the largest producer of bituminous coal in the country:

Indeed, there is no more striking human "landmark" of this section than "John Wright," who in the old days was often referred to as

Fig. 5.9. "Opening No. 202 Mine, Nov. 15, 1911." Tunnel construction is well underway and tracks have been laid.

the "Tall Sycamore of Elkhorn," and although now nearing his eightieth year, he is yet tall and straight, and is still an active and useful citizen; and in his rough dignity and friendly way, commands the respect and friendship of all. It was his "old homestead" upon which Jenkins was built, the Central office building standing where once stood his house and garden, and it was another of his "old homesteads" upon which McRoberts, our companion or twin town located across the mountain on Wright's Fork of Boone Creek, was erected. Seventeen years ago on a day of drizzling rain, the writer of this sketch riding horseback up Elkhorn, passing the Forks and going up Little Elkhorn through a swampy section, now the bed of Elkhorn Lake and Lakeside, remarked to his companions what a dismal place it was, little knowing that at the old farm house he had just passed there lived a man whose latch-string hung on the outside always, an open bid to come in and be fed and rested from your journey; one who could by his fireside, as he afterwards many times did, tell many a tale of quaint, unusual and stirring happenings of the earlier days in this section.

After recounting the adventures of various local residents, the author, in keeping with the company's practice of interpreting its own past in the most vainglorious of terms, recalls the first survey of the region:

> Later (1902) the same spot became "Camp Goodwater" with its fourteen tents of surveyors who were then locating the "Mineral lands" we are now mining; and still later, in the early fall of 1910, this famous Camping Ground of the earlier days became suddenly modernized by a two-night's visit of many capitalists and mining men then and now interested in the coal developments here. Fine men they were and a splendid camp they had. The big camp-fire in the center of the many white tents being surrounded by those fastidious men of the East, who for the most part being unaccustomed to such an unusual outing, were chatting and smoking and laughing, glad of this pleasant tho' strange break from the monotony of their city lives. They there touched the match that started the hum of this big mining industry, and, as the construction period is familiar to most of us, this brings us from where we started with this tale of "Jenkins Long Ago," up to the present time.[8]

Once these "fine men" had "touched the match," town construction and mine development were inaugurated. Holes were punched into the hillsides to make way for drift mines and, in time, slag heaps would become a prevalent feature throughout the hills and hollows (fig. 5.10). The region's forests and streams would never be the same. An insatiable demand for wood coupled with a need to secure an outlet for waste would see to that.

Felling the Forests

In 1963 the President's Appalachian Regional Commission (PARC) reported that proponents of sound timber resource management faced many serious challenges in Appalachia. Absentee control by extractive industries, fragmented ownership, rapid turnover, and sharply rising land prices near population centers were all identified as particularly vexing

Fig. 5.10. Here the drift mines appear to be overshadowed by the forested hillside.

problems. As a result, only "scattered remnants of quality timber" could be found within the "vast forest tracts of Appalachia." The PARC report stated that timber quality in Appalachia's forested lands was generally poor "because the forests have been 'creamed' again and again until in many areas, only the culls, small trees and undesirable species are left." The photographs selected for this portion of the chapter communicate to the reader in no uncertain terms just what the contributors to the PARC report meant by that statement.[9]

In 1926 the *Mutual Monthly* reported, "When in 1910 The Consolidation Coal Company purchased 100,000 acres of coal lands in Pike, Letcher, and Knott Counties, Kentucky, it found these lands a wilderness of virgin forests which were inhabited by mountaineers" (fig. 5.11). As the photograph and supporting caption in figure 5.12 confirms, it did not take long for the company to begin clearing the forest. Historically, commercial coal mine operators routinely removed all overlying timber before

Fig. 5.11. "Large Trees, Bark Camp Branch, 6/12/12." Some of the forests company surveyors encountered—especially in eastern Kentucky and southern West Virginia—were truly ancient.

Fig. 5.12. "Cutting Timber, Elkhorn Forest, April 1, 1912."

the process of mining was begun. As one forester put it in 1900, "Wherever coal lands bearing considerable useful timber are controlled by ownership, the usual plan is to remove all usable timber before the coal is mined. This takes all sound trees down to about three inches in diameter." During the nineteenth and early twentieth centuries, most mine operators across the country adopted the attitude that "forests that hindered mining should be removed." Where control of natural resources fell into the hands of large coal corporations, it is easy to imagine the rapidity with which large tracts were deforested.[10]

Forests were not leveled simply because they stood in the way of mine preparation. The establishment of a new mining operation required vast quantities of wood for a variety of purposes. Timber was cut and sawed into lumber to be used in the construction of houses, outbuildings, tipples, trestles, and other structures associated with mining (fig. 5.13). Wood was also fashioned into mining props and railroad crossties. The demand for mine props was especially strong. In 1900, for example, an official in the Forestry Division at the U.S. Department of Agriculture conducted a survey of forest resources in western Maryland—birthplace of the Consolidation Coal Company—and estimated that roughly one million props were being cut per year to serve the coal and fire-clay mines of Allegany County. At the time, this represented an annual culling of approximately twenty-eight thousand acres. Nine years later, a Maryland State Board of Forestry report determined that one million mine props and forty-seven thousand railroad ties were being consumed each year in Allegany County. The magnitude of the problem comes into sharp focus when one bears in mind that before the widespread use of chemical preservatives such as coal-tar creosote, crossties had to be replaced every six to seven years. With an average of 2,640 crossties per mile of track, it was not unusual to find broad stretches of denuded land on either side of the railroad bed. Writing in 1927, Nelson Courtlandt Brown, professor of forest utilization at Syracuse University, singled out Pennsylvania as the greatest consumer of lumber and timbers, calculating that the state probably purchased "more than 50 per cent of the total value of mine timbers used in the entire country."[11]

The impact that advances in cutting technology had on forest resources cannot be overlooked. Over time, the ax and whipsaw gave way to more efficient water-powered saws, which, in turn, eventually gave way to steam-powered circular saws and band saws capable of cutting sixty to

Fig. 5.13. "Mine No. 7 Hoist House and Timber Yard."

eighty thousand board feet per day. The adoption of these newer saws greatly accelerated the rate at which the forests could be cut. More significant, the portable circular and band saws permitted cutting to take place in areas far removed from a source of water power. As these figures from 1918 affirm, Consolidation applied the most modern means to produce its own props, ties, and lumber:

> In the Elkhorn Division, The Consolidation Coal Company operates its own saw-mills. There are three of these mills in this division, with a total capacity of 360,000 feet of lumber per month. They employ 85 men. When mill No. 14 began operation about six months ago, the estimate of lumber, near Haymond, where this mill is located, was about 6,000,000 feet. During the first six months, the output of lumber at this mill was 1,250,000 feet, leaving more than 5,000,000 feet to be cut, as the output will always exceed the estimate. At mill No. 1, near Mine No. 203, 35 men were employed, and 2,020,000 feet of lumber manufactured.

Fig. 5.14. "New logging locomotive purchased for the Forestry Department to work a tract of timber, the estimated area of which is 22,000 acres." CCC *Mutual Monthly Magazine,* July–August 1926, 49.

The introduction of narrow-gauge logging railroads and loading equipment also served to step up the pace of cutting (fig. 5.14).[12]

Browsing the pages of the company magazine, one can detect a shift in thinking on the part of editors and contributors with respect to forest resources. As serviceable timber started to become scarce in some locales, and therefore more valuable, an increased emphasis was placed on extending the life of mine props and cross ties, as the following entry from 1928 indicates:

The life of mine timber can be increased indefinitely by a thorough preservative treatment, provided that the timbers are not broken by pressure or destroyed by mechanical wear. The best record of service noted in this investigation consisted of shaft timbers given a pressure treatment with creosote; these have been in service 18 years

and are still in a sound condition. Other installations of treated
mine timber show a life of 15 to 18 years, with the material not yet
tested to failure by decay. . . . The fundamental principle of mine
timber treatment is to treat the inferior and cheaper grades of timber and to use them wherever possible as a substitute for the more
costly and more enduring grades, which may have to be imported
from other States.

The reference to importation of timber from other states is an important
one. While it underscores the need to take advantage of chemical preservatives, it also hints at the fact that some tree species of a particular quality were, in fact, becoming scarce.[13]

In the same story, after pointing out that readjustment of ventilating
systems to introduce more fresh air may discourage decay, the author dis-
cusses the advantages of wood preservatives. He points out that the wood
must be prepared for treatment by stripping the bark and seasoning the
wood, as bark is all but impervious to preservatives and green wood is
resistant to the injection of the necessary chemicals. In general, pressure
treatments with alternating hot and cold baths were considered more efficient than dipping and brush treatments. Only some timbers were recommended for treatment, however. In general, permanent and semipermanent
timbers—shaft and slope timbers, entry timbers, main and secondary
motor-track ties, wooden tipples and head frames, trestles, poles, and
crossties—were recommended for treatment. It was not considered economically worthwhile to treat room ties, room props, mine-car timber,
and other miscellaneous timber.[14]

The Forestry Division's report on western Maryland, mentioned earlier in this section, came up with several recommendations for the recovery of the region's forested areas. These included protecting the remaining
forests from fire, excluding grazing from forest lands, and regulating indis-
criminate cutting and clearing. Nevertheless, the report made it abun-
dantly clear that certain priorities had to be recognized and followed: "The
much greater value of the coal deposit must always properly have prece-
dence over the present timber crop lying above, and also over that which
would have been possible during the term of years necessary for the land
to recuperate from the effects of the undermining." It was an attitude that
must have been standard among many landowners, individual or corporate, who possessed large stands of timber underlain by deposits of coal.[15]

Trees took on much greater value in the mining towns themselves. Indeed, planting trees for beautification was held in high regard:

You will notice that the substantial, the thrifty, the worthy, and the likable classes of people plant trees, no matter whether they are in a new and treeless country or in one already well planted; and that the shiftless, the transient, the careless, and the selfish are as little likely to set out sheltering trees as they are to be neat, thrifty, or good neighbors. Show me a developed town with no trees and I will show you a town to avoid as a home for your families. Go through districts where want and squalor and crime and filth are the rule and you will be lucky to find even a gaunt specimen of a tree anywhere about. This is not by chance; the planted and tended tree is [as sure a] sign of civilization as a revered flag or a church spire or a schoolhouse belfry, and the English, who have carried civilization to every part of their dominions scattered far and wide about the earth, plant shade trees almost before they finish their houses or start their towns.

Nowhere is the distinction between a "timber crop" located on the out-skirts of town and trees planted for shade in the mining community made so unmistakably than in this passage from a 1928 issue of the *Mutual Monthly* (fig. 5.15).[16]

As Consolidation Coal opened up new areas to coal mining in Penn-sylvania, West Virginia, and Kentucky after the turn of the twentieth cen-tury, it is possible to discern regional shifts in attitude with respect to mining and its impact on the physical environment. After more than fifty years of large-scale mining activity, the forest and water resources in the vicinity of the Georges Creek valley in Allegany County, Maryland, had been devastated (fig. 5.16). As a result, both the Maryland Geological Sur-vey and the State Board of Forestry endorsed the idea that the state should acquire lands in this region to ensure recovery. The attitude that prevailed in Kentucky some twenty years later could not have been more different. According to a 1927 report by state geologist Willard Rouse Jillson, "The progress of Kentucky is . . . plainly bound up in the development of its mineral and natural resource wealth of all kinds, and the founding upon this natural wealth of a large resident manufacturing industry. . . . Ken-tucky needs to arouse herself to a critical situation. Definite and well directed action should be taken to invite invested wealth into its borders."[17]

Fig. 5.15. "Jenkins Main Street Looking East 5-8-30."

Fig. 5.16. "Mine No. 7 from Dirt Dump."

Noting that only 51 percent of the state had been accurately mapped to date, Jillson admonished Kentuckians to support expenditures of "energy and money, carefully systematizing and grouping the natural resources of large areas" of the state. To Jillson, the justification for supporting a project such as this was obvious: "No corporation or individual could hope to succeed today in the face of great competition with the utilization of only about 51 percent. of its resources." To this end, he urged that topographers and economic geologists "comb the hills and vales of every unmapped county" in search of natural resources. Such unabashed boosterism was not uncommon among state resource personnel at the time. Truth be told, many were in a position to benefit from the new development.[18]

What impact did the coal mining industry have on Appalachia's forests? Perhaps Peter Roberts, whose work in the early years of the twentieth century focused on the anthracite coal region of northeastern Pennsylvania, has left us with the most eloquent explanation: "A great change has come over this charming landscape. The hills have been stripped of their forests and the major part of the graceful trees which once bent to the storm now rot in the caves of the earth, where, for a time, they afforded protection to mine employees engaged in digging coal."[19]

Impacts to Water

Historically, coal-mining activities have taken a severe toll on the region's water resources as well. Waters issuing from abandoned mines are often very acidic and laden with high concentrations of metals such as iron, manganese, and aluminum. If permitted to come into contact with surface waters, this discharge, known as acid mine drainage, or AMD, "can destroy natural habitats, pollute surface and groundwater resources, endanger nearby populations, and result in the deterioration of the natural aesthetic environment." It is also very difficult and costly to clean up. Given the practices of the day and the proximity of the mines to local streams in some areas, the impact was largely unavoidable (fig. 5.17). As the images in this section disclose, problems associated with abundance and relative scarcity of water presented the company with serious challenges.[20]

One observer has remarked that, "Water, one of nature's principal blessings, is a boon to most industries, but in coal mining it is a constant source of expense and trouble," for it often severely limits access to coal deposits. To mitigate this problem, hundreds of miles of drainage ditches

Fig. 5.17. Mine No. 1 in western Maryland.

and tunnels were constructed throughout Consolidation's properties. Included among these projects was the two-mile gravity-flow Hoffman Drainage Tunnel in western Maryland (fig. 5.18). Constructed between 1903 and 1906, the Hoffman Tunnel eventually received water from thirteen miles of drainage ditches. As historian Jeanne Cordts comments, "A tremendous reserve of coal heretofore unavailable was now accessible. With the water level down, working conditions improved and output of coal increased dramatically." Needless to say, engineering feats such as the Hoffman Tunnel, or the two-mile Jack Run Drainage Ditch in West Virginia, increased the output of sulfuric acid entering nearby streams.[21]

Although the negative environmental impacts of acid mine drainage were well known before the turn of the twentieth century, streams and rivers continued to receive acid backwash from the mines, often for decades. Degradation of streams continued thanks in large part to a landmark Pennsylvania Supreme Court case in 1886, *Pennsylvania Coal*

Fig. 5.18. The Hoffman Drainage Tunnel in western Maryland.

Co. v. Sanderson, in which the plaintiff argued that acid mine drainage had killed all the fish in a downstream tributary and prevented him from using the water. The court ruled that the mine drainage did not constitute a private nuisance: "mere private personal inconveniences . . . must yield to the necessities of a great public industry. . . . To encourage the development of the great natural resources of a country trifling inconveniences to particular persons must sometimes give way." William J. Gerlach reminds us that this case was not "expressly overruled until 1974."[22]

Pennsylvania Coal's victory is all the more impressive when we take into account the manner in which it prevailed in this case:

> The famous case, *Sanderson v. Pennsylvania Coal Co.,* is an example of powerful polluters continuing to litigate until judges adopted rules that favored their interests. The Sanderson plaintiffs sued a coal company for damages to compensate them for harm done their rural estate by the defendant's coal mine, which was poisoning their water supply. After an appeals court reversed the trial-court decision to dismiss the case, in the process granting damages, the coal company appealed the case four more times, twice before the Pennsylvania Supreme Court. The coal company continued to lose on appeal, with a majority of the judges, including those who heard the case in the Supreme Court, repeatedly upholding the decision to award the plaintiffs damages. The defendant won the case only by using its vast resources to keep litigating until the membership of the Pennsylvania Supreme Court changed. Finally, on the fifth appeal, after the installation of a new justice, the Supreme Court adopted new rules that justified applying the catastrophic economic domino-effect reasoning of balancing to damage cases of this ilk. This legitimized the denial of any and all relief to the plaintiffs.

As Christine M. Rosen has shown, polluting businesses in Pennsylvania were often the beneficiaries of a state judicial system that generally favored big business. Even when unfavorable decisions were handed down, the coal industry had the financial wherewithal to pursue the matter in the courts indefinitely, ostensibly to present its case but more likely biding its time until a change of circumstances permitted a more advantageous outcome. Perhaps the precedent that was established in this case should be looked upon as the true measure of the ascendancy of King Coal.[23]

By no means was the coal industry the only offender when it came to water pollution during this period. In addition to the acid waters emanating from the mines, wastes from tanneries, slaughterhouses, and paper mills fouled waters across the region. Depending on the community and local economy, wastes from breweries, distilleries, and sundry other businesses were also dispensed to surface waters. Of course, domestic refuse and sewage made their way to these same "sinks" as well. By the 1890s, if not earlier in some areas, newspapers and state and federal government documents were reporting on the poor condition of Appalachia's (and other regions') water courses. In 1897, for instance, a survey of the Potomac River basin conducted by the U. S. Department of the Interior concluded that Georges Creek, the principal stream flowing through western Maryland's coal-mining region,

> is badly polluted, the iron oxide being precipitated on the bowlders
> [*sic*] in the creek and lending to the whole stream a rust-colored
> appearance. In its course through Westernport it assumes much the
> nature of a public sewer. Refuse of every description is dumped into
> it; two slaughterhouses drain into it, and along its entire course
> through the town it receives the sewage from a double series of priv-
> ies. . . . At Lonaconing the bed of the creek is strewed with debris
> and rubbish of all sorts.

Newspaper accounts tended to be more graphic in their descriptions of polluted waters, providing details on color, odor, floating debris, and effects on aquatic life. While their waste disposal practices were really no different from other industries—they all dumped their wastes into nearby streams—coal companies, by virtue of the enormous volume of acid drainage and other wastes they handled, had a far greater impact on the region's surface waters.[24]

Again, testimony from Peter Roberts is revealing. Referring to the anthracite region of Pennsylvania he states:

> The waters of nearly 400 collieries impregnated with sulphur, flow-
> ing into the creeks and rivers have killed the fish. In addition to this,
> the necessity in recent years of washing the coal before sending it to
> market as well as the erection of washeries for the overhauling of the
> culm heaps, adds to every available stream a quantity of foul water
> laden with coal dust which turns the creeks and rivers into a mass of
> black flowing stuff that is a curse to all forms of organic life.

As other sources have shown, some of the worst pollution came not from the mines but the mining communities themselves: "To this defilement of the streams another still more poisonous defilement is added. The towns and cities located on the banks of these creeks and rivers turn the contents of their sewers into them. This pollution imperils the health of mining communities themselves. In some regions the streams are little better than open sewers contaminating the air with poisonous gases."[25]

Occasionally, even the *Mutual Monthly* would publish a letter or note from one of its mining communities that would refer—if only very vaguely and indirectly—to problems relating to water pollution. Such statements were rare and generally benign. In 1925, for example, came this entry from Mine No. 38 in West Virginia: "During the month of September the water of Buffalo Creek became very low and stagnant. As a consequence hundreds of the cat fish in the stream died. Heavy rains in October were more than welcome to the inhabitants of creek and present indications are that there will be no more stagnant water in Buffalo Creek until next summer at least." From Mine No. 120 in Pennsylvania came this far more optimistic note: "A shipment of 5,000 brook trout was received by the Acosta Sportsmen's Association and placed in our . . . streams in this vicinity. Another shipment of fish is expected to arrive in the near future." How long the fish would survive in streams subjected to the effects of acid mine drainage, not to mention the refuse and effluent of numerous other sources, is difficult to say.[26]

Today, acid waters issuing from abandoned mines have rendered lifeless thousands of miles of streams in Appalachia. The magnitude of the problem can best be seen in the following figures for Pennsylvania during 1920–21. Some twelve hundred operating coal mines drained an estimated 450 million tons of water that year, containing nearly 1.6 million tons of sulfuric acid. Add to that the large number of abandoned mines—estimates of which ran as high as six thousand—and the extent of the environmental challenge today comes into sharp focus.[27]

In figures 5.19 and 5.20 we see that Consolidation Coal found it necessary at times to impound water. In some cases reservoirs were constructed to provide a source of drinking water for the mining community; in other cases, dams were built with power production in mind. The company satisfied both these needs when it built a dam across the narrow gorge of little Elkhorn Creek near Jenkins, Kentucky, thus, in Beachley's words, "creating a beautiful lake of some fifteen acres picturesquely nestled at the foot of the surrounding hills." As mines penetrated deeper and

Fig. 5.19. "Little Elkhorn Reservoir Basin August 16, 1911." This photo was taken before the construction of the reservoir on this site (fig. 5.20).

Fig. 5.20. "Elkhorn Lake, Jenkins, Ky."

deeper into the hills and more sophisticated equipment was applied to the mine site, electricity had to be generated to support the needs of the miners. Thus, in addition to serving as a reservoir, the company's coal-fired power plant used water from the lake to make steam to generate electricity for use in the mines and by the mining community. If the state geological survey's W. R. King had had his way, Kentucky might have taken even greater advantage of the region's rivers and streams. Writing in 1924, King made a case for developing Kentucky's water resources even further: "Those who have investigated the extent of our natural resources realize that the supply of coal and oil is not inexhaustible. The rapid depletion of the supply of coal is strikingly illustrated by the fact that 800,000,000 tons of coal were mined in the United States in 1920. The demand upon oil is also heavy. It is therefore essential to conserve the supply of both coal and oil by the development of water power wherever such development is economically possible."[28]

Aftermath

In a promotional brochure published in 1989, the Consolidation Coal Company reflected on its more than 120 years of coal-mining history and concluded that the opening of the mines in Appalachia "brought new life and purpose to the land. Mining towns like Monongah in northern West Virginia, Jenner in west-central Pennsylvania and Jenkins in eastern Kentucky developed a sense of pioneer spirit, a sense of harvesting the land's resources to build a better America." The statement is as ironic as it is revealing. Clearly a new purpose *was* brought to the land, one that favored a "materialistic and entirely utilitarian view of natural resources"; one that championed economic progress regardless of the environmental cost; one that placed a premium on short-term monetary gain. As the images on display in this chapter verify, however, we would be pressing the outer limits of hyperbole if we were to conclude that mining "brought new life" to the land. Indeed, quite the opposite was true.[29]

That a "utilitarian view of natural resources" was gaining widespread acceptance among Americans can be affirmed by their staid reactions to the environmental changes that were taking place all around them, but also by the business rhetoric of the period. As one might expect, a utilitarian view of natural resources was embraced and promoted by key members of the business community. In his address to the West Virginia University Business Club, for example, Stephen Q. Hayes, general engineer of the Westinghouse Electric and Manufacturing Company, asserted that West Virginia was "primarily a fuel state, probably the greatest fuel state in America," as it possessed "a splendid market for its production as well as the resources to supply such a market." At a dinner of the West Virginia Lumber and Builders' Supply Dealers, Frank Roy Yoke, alumni secretary of West Virginia University, adopted a similar approach:

> I am here tonight to refute some of the libels that have been per-
> petuated upon this state we all love. I want to tell you some of the
> reasons and some of the things that make me happy to be a West
> Virginian. It is said, and it is true, there are but three torches of
> progress: coal, oil and gas. West Virginia is the most important
> coal producing state within the union. She has 85 seams of coal,
> 49 counties underlaid by these seams. In 1920, she produced
> 99,000,000 tons of coal and still has enough coal at that rate of
> production to last 1600 years. . . . Thirty-one of West Virginia's
> counties produce oil of a high grade. In 1920, West Virginia pro-
> duced two-fifths of all the gas produced in the United States of
> America, and yet, possessing these three great torches of progress,
> the eastern press dares to say that we are an island of barbarity
> surrounded by a sea of civilization.

Both Hayes and Yoke go on to discuss the state's mineral wealth, as well as its various industries, its transportation infrastructure, agricultural production, and "patriotism."[30]

By the late nineteenth century, coal-mining technology was capable of completely reworking the physical landscape. Within thirty years, Appalachia's coal boom would grind to a halt. The "pioneer spirit" that companies like Consolidation purport to have brought to the mountains would all but erode in the face of the Great Depression. To historian Jerry Bruce Thomas, "the lumber and coal industries, after having heedlessly denuded mountains and polluted the streams, passed their peaks as employers, leaving stranded families the choice of using the new roads as escape routes to jobs in industrial centers or struggling to make a living from their mountain farms."[31]

Extracting Appalachia

"Take me," Father was saying. "I never tuck natural to growing things, planting seeds and sticking plows in the ground like Taulbee Lovern. A furrow I run allus did crook like a black-snake's track. A sight of farming I've done, but it allus rubbed the grain. But give me a pick, and I'll dig as much coal as the next 'un. I figure them mines won't stay closed forever."

—James Still, *River of Earth,* 1940

God made the coal and he hid it. Then some fool found it, and we've been in trouble ever since.

—*United Mine Workers Journal,* 1976

By now it should be obvious to the reader that photographs are not neutral transcriptions of fact:

> Conventional wisdom would have it that photographs transmit immutable truths. But although the very notion of photographic reproduction would seem to suggest that very little is lost in translation, it is clear that photographic meaning depends largely on context. Despite the powerful impression of reality (imparted by the mechanical registration of a moment of reflected light according to the rules of normal perspective), photographs are fragmentary and incomplete utterances. . . . Clearly archives are not neutral; they embody the power inherent in accumulation, collection, and hoarding as well as that power inherent in the command of the lexicon and rules of a language.

Why were the photographs in the Smithsonian archive taken and for whom were they intended? What do they tell us about life and labor in a company town? About the coal industry in Appalachia? About social and economic conditions across the region? About the company that made them? It is to these questions and others that we now turn our attention.[1]

Browsing the photographs in the collection, it is clear that different portions served different purposes and were intended for different audiences. Pictures of miners at work and at rest, group pictures of employees engaged in other activities for the company, winners of garden contests, team and school portraits, picnics and holiday celebrations, as well as churches, recreational facilities, store merchandise, and miners' houses, were published regularly in the company's magazine, the *CCC Mutual Monthly,* and included in the company's photo albums. Their purpose was to instill a sense of belonging and to promote community spirit. Images of safety demonstrations, steel timbers, miners using equipment the "right way" and the "wrong way"—photographs which are best understood in relation to the Monongah disaster of 1907—were probably used to train new miners and to impress mine inspectors. These photos were also intended for a general audience and were featured prominently in the company albums.

While the company may have taken a genuine interest in the health and safety of its workers, it must be remembered that maintaining a high level of production was of paramount importance. Thus the photos were sent directly to the miners via the pages of the company journal. Images of mine accidents, overturned locomotives, striking workers, and violent clashes were maintained for company records and insurance or legal purposes, but it is doubtful they were distributed widely or placed in albums for public display (fig. 6.1). And, of course, there were pictures of the company's product: coal. Two-inch, four-inch, and six-inch lump; two-inch and four-inch modified; two-by-four-inch and six-by-four-inch egg; nut; and run-of-mine—the company had photographic samples of each (figs. 6.2, 6.3). No doubt these were shown to prospective customers.

Many of the images in the albums and magazine are of machinery and equipment, much of which was state-of-the-art. While they may have been taken primarily for insurance reasons, it is also obvious company officials were proud of the new machines and devices that were allowing its miners to remove more coal faster than the competition; the new equipment was revolutionizing the industry. Even the introduction of a new tipple—a commonplace feature of any coal-mining site—could

Fig. 6.1. "201 Slide—Burried [*sic*] Locomotive. 2-4-23."

generate enthusiasm, as this caption to a photograph in the November 1918 issue of the *Mutual Monthly* shows:

> The photograph here reproduced is of the tipple at Mine No. 40. This tipple was put in operation on August 19, 1918, replacing the one destroyed by fire during the year 1916. The present tipple is a steel structure with a frame cover; it was transferred from Mine No. 28 which was abandoned some years ago. The new tipple is doing good work; it is equipped with a shaker screen and is designed for handling approximately three tons of coal per minute. Three grades of coal can be loaded over the tipple: slack [finest screenings of coal], nut and three-quarters. The tipple also includes a run of mine chute and is in every way up-to-date.[2]

Perhaps more so than other photographs in the collection, those associated with environmental alteration must be placed in historical context.

Fig. 6.2. Coal from "Mine No. 206—8-15-26."

Fig. 6.3. "Car of 2" Modified—Mine No. 206—8-12-26."

Paul Nyden has remarked, "A malevolent Midas, King Coal devastates what it touches"; the photographs focused on this theme clearly support this contention. That they were exhibited in the leather-bound albums suggests company officials wanted to maintain a record of mine development and progress (fig. 6.4). The before and after shots, in particular, remind us of what existed before large-scale transformation took place. In some cases, the juxtaposition of old and new provides a fascinating, even disturbing, study in contrasts (fig. 6.5). The photos in this section are also valuable because they show us how human settlement adapted to local conditions and how company decisions actually played out on the surface. At a minimum, we catch a glimpse of the tremendous force that the coal-mining industry brought to bear on the hills and hollows of Appalachia. That scenes of despoliation did not engender a powerful and enduring resistance movement is indicative of the power and influence the coal industry enjoyed at the time and, as Brian Black asserts, the tolerance many Americans were willing to exercise when confronted by such images: "The moral here is simple: leave it to Americans to make the most of their natural resources. Such confidence in one's culture and society truly drove the pistons of industrial development and allowed Americans to become comfortable with and even excited by dramatic shifts in land use." Mining landscapes were not, in Richard Francaviglia's words, "held in disdain." Quite the opposite. "To Victorians, they may even have epitomized civilization's inevitable victory in the quest for knowledge and superiority over nature."[3]

If there is one point that emerges from even a superficial examination of the photographs, it is that Consolidation Coal took great pride in all it had accomplished. The company was proud that it was building towns considered a cut above other mining communities, proud of its record of mine safety in the years after the Monongah disaster, and proud of its investment in advanced technology. Company officials, photographers, writers, editors, and salesmen likely had a greater purpose in mind when they made and distributed these photographs, however. In reference to the appeal and authority of the photographs in the General Electric collection, David Nye comments: "Each photograph seems prototypically real, a replica of something indisputably actual. Because photographs have this quality, they proved uniquely well suited to the corporation's need to address many audiences, giving its messages the aura of fact." Hence the value of the photos to the Consolidation Coal Company when it came to convincing government inspectors and legislators they were doing every-

Fig. 6.4. "Working on Railroad at Joe's Branch, Sept. 18, 1911." The arrival of the railroad to a coal-mining district usually signaled the start of large-scale coal mining.

thing in their power to insure the safety of workers and that strict new mine safety laws were not necessary. Even more important, they could be employed to convince shareholders and potential investors that the coal business was viable and that a "model city" was being constructed in the mountains of eastern Kentucky. According to Jon M. Williams and Daniel T. Muir, the DuPont Corporation tapped photographs for the same purpose: "It was evidently felt that a picture, even a sketch, would be more reassuring than a verbal description." When viewed in this light, photographs were powerful devices in the hands of company officials.[4]

Explicit and Implicit Landscapes

As numerous scholars over the years have argued, there is more to photographs than meets the eye. In a sense, all the photos in the Smithsonian

Fig. 6.5. "Old & New Houses—No. 203 Mine. April 1, 1912."

collection reveal two sets of landscapes. Hidden beneath the readily apparent, or explicit, landscapes of the built environment are deeper, less conspicuous, implicit landscapes. These implicit landscapes conceal contemporary societal attitudes, values, and ethics. If investigated carefully, they
also disclose corporate designs and intentions.

To begin with, wherever we look we are reminded of the wealth and
power of the company. The wealth of Consolidation Coal manifests itself
most noticeably in the pictures of paved streets and town construction. It
is clear that the company was investing considerable sums of money in an
infrastructure that was intended to last. In some towns at least, Consolidation was providing more than the bare essentials. They were building
churches, stores, recreational facilities, and other "amenities" that smaller
companies simply could not afford to build. Likewise, photos of trains
overflowing with coal and brand-new equipment remind us of the company's impressive financial base. As William Graebner points out, even

health and safety photographs can be interpreted as an indication of a company's wealth:

> United States Steel Corporation, in the forefront of the movement to extirpate unions, also employed the most advanced safety measures and systems in its coal-mining subsidiaries. . . . United States Steel's interest in safety was also consistent with the company's size. The larger coal companies, with their superior financial resources and greater overhead, were usually the ones to institute employee representation and other programs of more exclusively safety content. Only the larger companies could consider placing telephones in the mines; finance their own scientific investigations of safety problems; send men to Europe to study modern methods of conservation and accident prevention . . . ; or publish safety literature in several languages.

Finally, the company's sponsorship of baseball teams and special events, such as this miners' picnic in 1926, provide further evidence of Consol's abundant resources: "On September 4th, The Consolidation Coal Company gave an all day picnic at Jenkins for the employees of the Elkhorn Division. The number of people in attendance was estimated at seven thousand. . . . The program included many athletic events, miscellaneous contests, and ended with a ball game in the afternoon in which the Jenkins Team defeated Hazard by the close score of 7 to 6." According to the *Mutual Monthly*, "the entire expenses of the day were borne by The Consolidation Coal Company."[5]

At first glance, one cannot help but be impressed by the degree to which the coal camps and mining operations left their stamp on the physical environment. The photographs are striking. If we keep in mind the commercial nature of the images, however, we can view the landscapes of town construction and environmental transformation they represent as more than simply verification of changes taking place on a local scale in a remote section of the country. We can see them as part of a much larger picture—one in which coal towns were enmeshed in a web of social and economic flows, interactions, and relations. The deforested hills, contaminated streams, gob piles, and trash heaps provide undeniable evidence of Appalachia's position in the national economy. As such, they are reflections of human values and priorities; artifacts that cause us to recollect how we defined, used, and valued natural resources at a specific point in time. On this point Donald Meinig's words are apropos: "Where those

Fig. 6.6. "Battle Royal at Miners Picnic—9-4-26."

who see landscape as problem see disorder, clutter, incongruity, conges-
tion, pollution, sprawl, and dereliction amid the glitter, those who see it
as ideology may see distinct manifestations of American interpretations
of freedom, individualism, competition, utility, power, modernity, expansion, progress." The statement rings as true today with respect to our
treatment of natural resources as it did a quarter century ago.[6]

By openly espousing the principles of "Americanism"—stressing the
importance of law and order, obedience to employer, and loyalty to country, Consolidation's Employment Relationship Department was engaged
in a conscious effort to influence the behavior of the company's workforce. In his book *The Americanization of West Virginia*, John C. Hennen
writes, "Industrial Americanizers of 1916–25, employing the vocabulary
of democracy, embraced a social model in which order and efficiency
superceded social and economic justice and sought to legitimate their
claim to rule by narrowing the field of tolerable discourse, dissent, and
alternatives to industrial capitalism." In a very real sense, the photographs
in the Consolidation Coal collection abetted the Employment Relation-

ship Department's efforts to achieve the company's goals. When we gaze at rows of freshly painted company houses, merchandise at the company store, group photos of miners, and impressive gardens, we must ask ourselves why the company selected these images for publication in its magazine. We must recall that company towns were carefully planned places designed to maximize production and enhance surveillance. We must remember the company store's reputation—deserved or not—for price gouging and debt peonage. We must keep in mind that group photographs were often taken to promote a sense of belonging and camaraderie among residents. David Corbin argues that coal companies even had a hidden agenda when it came to gardens:

> Encouraging miners to grow gardens and to upgrade their houses was certainly an effort on the part of the company to occupy their employees' spare time, the misuse of which was the cause of labor trouble; one coal operator declared: 'There are two schools of miners, those who expend their surplus time and energy in fighting and those who use it for gardening.' Prizes for gardening and homes also had, undoubtedly, other purposes. At a minimal cost to the company (e.g., a twenty-dollar gold piece per year), the operators could impart in the miner a pride in his yard and in his house, although he owned neither. It was, furthermore, a cheap means of upgrading the physical environment of the town, and, most important, it stimulated neighborly (social) competition in a rigidly ordered social structure.

Even seemingly innocent photographs of miners and their families enjoying themselves at a company-sponsored picnic can, upon closer inspection, present us with some troubling questions. For instance, the participants in the "Battle Royal" at the Elkhorn Division's picnic are all African American men (fig. 6.6). Unlike other events and contests, there appears to have been no comparable event for white males. Perhaps that means nothing. On the other hand, it may speak volumes about race and ethnicity in early-twentieth-century America.[7]

"Certain Absences"

In reference to a historical pictorial lithograph of Syracuse, New York, geographer Rich Schein offered the following cautionary note: "The viewer of this scene—past and present—would be well served by the

advice to 'be haunted by certain absences' in picturesque representations."
Close examination of the Consolidation Coal photographs reveals that
one should resist the temptation to conclude that they somehow tell the
whole story when it comes to coal mining in Appalachia during the first
half of the twentieth century. As with the lithograph of Syracuse, readers
of the Consol photographs should be troubled by "certain absences." By
comparing the photographs in the Smithsonian collection with images in
the federal government's Farm Security Administration (FSA) file, as well
as photos in the Mary Behner Christopher collection at West Virginia University, we get a feel for what some of those absences are. Regardless of
who is responsible for making the photograph, we are left, in the end, to
ponder just what images the miners and their families would have chosen
to include in the company's albums had they been presented with such an
opportunity.[8]

So what do these photographs *not* show us? With the exception of a
small album of photographs showing United Mine Workers' marches and
strikes in the Fairmont region of West Virginia during 1932, union activity is largely omitted. This is somewhat surprising, given the space devoted
to the topic in the company magazine. Besides one potent image of a
black miner being restrained by two policemen (fig. 4.24), violent conflicts
between striking miners and scabs or between workers and mine guards
are conspicuously absent. Evidence of economic or social strife during the
Depression is nonexistent. There is no indication that thousands of miners were joining the ranks of the unemployed, that families in some coalfields were on the verge of starvation, that Consol itself would file for
bankruptcy in 1932.

Similarly, we never see the interiors of company-owned houses. Nor are
we able to observe the material possessions of the mining families or witness the domestic labor of women and children. In fact, except for photos
of public celebrations such as miners' picnics and garden contests, of the
occasional visiting nurse or schoolteacher, or of the picket line, women
are not well represented in the Smithsonian collection. Clearly, the world
of coal mining was dominated by men. Employment opportunities for
women outside the home were few: "Actually, outside of school teaching,
there were few paying jobs available for women, and those available were
primarily in the needle trades or laundries. . . . Ironically these industries
also required the longest work days, and West Virginia was one of four
states that neither placed limits on women's hours nor provided any pro-
tective legislation for working women." Writing of the Depression era in

West Virginia, Jerry Bruce Thomas notes that with more than one-third of farmers working for wages off the farm, including in the mines, women and children were left to do most of the farmwork. In addition they were responsible for "feeding and watering stock, carrying wood or coal, carrying water from the spring, and hoeing and raking, as well as the customary house chores such as cooking, washing, and child care." One could easily make the argument that the life of a woman in a company town was every bit as difficult as that of a miner: "Miners' wives bore heavy burdens not only literally but psychologically. They faced the insecurities of life in the coal country, where the threat of death or serious injury to the male breadwinner loomed over the family. Between 1897 and 1928, more than ten thousand men died in West Virginia's coal mines, a rate of more than 330 per year, and in 1928 alone 475 died." As the women featured in Carol A. B. Giesen's book *Coal Miners' Wives* clearly stated, "no one but a miner's wife could understand the stresses of a miner's wife."[9]

Comparing the pictures in the Consol collection with images taken by Farm Security Administration photographers, as well as those found in private collections such as the Mary Behner Christopher archive, we find sharp differences with respect to content. Unlike the Consol photographers, the FSA photographers show us the grim side of life in a coal-mining town—the unpaved streets, the poor condition of company housing, the inadequate facilities for drinking water and for waste disposal. The government photos, in particular, remind us that it was not uncommon to find children working in and around the mines. Government photographers also take us into the homes of the miners so that we can view the condition of company-owned houses and gain valuable insights into the daily lives of the mining families. Photos in the Mary Behner Christopher collection present us with similar imagery. Especially evocative are photographs showing children lined up to receive a free hot meal—a poignant reminder of the desperate economic predicament in which many miners' families found themselves.

Thus we are presented with two very different portraits of coal mining in Appalachia. Is one more "truthful" or "objective" than the other? To be sure, each was developed with a different purpose in mind. Clearly, the overarching purpose of the company albums and the company magazine was to project a positive image of Consolidation's operations to individuals and groups unable to participate in the "mining" experience firsthand. However, the photos offer only a sanitized version of life in Appalachia's coalfields. The towns we see are model towns. It is not clear whether they are representative of conditions at other Consolidation locations. With respect to Appalachia as a whole, they appear to be the exception rather than the rule. While the photos reveal patterns of material culture and town layout, they only hint at the social, ethnic, and socioeconomic patterns associated with these communities, and the segregation and corporate paternalism that was characteristic of the period. The photographs in the Consolidation collection were not taken to strike an emotional chord, to shame an affluent society, or advance the cause of social reform as, say, Lewis Hine's work for the National Child Labor Committee did during the first two decades of the twentieth century. These photographs served the needs of the company. Any attempt to make generalizations about life and labor across the region based on their content would ultimately prove futile.[10]

Of course, certain aspects of life in a coal town can never truly be conveyed in a photograph, regardless of who makes it. According to retired Consol miner Robert Armstead, "Anytime I went outside, even in the winter, I inhaled the foul smells of Grays Flats and Grant Town. Every yard had an outdoor toilet, and in the hot summer, they smelled horrible. Each spring the coal company paid Luke Anderson, a black man, to clean all the outside toilets. The heavy odor of human waste gagged us and clung to our clothes for days after he 'honey-dipped' the toilets." And then there was the smoke. Because coal was used to generate power and to heat homes, smoke was everywhere present in the atmosphere (see fig. 6.6). Returning to Armstead's personal account:

> I lived my entire childhood breathing in smoke and the stench
> of burning coal. The smell resembled scorched linen. Day and night
> we smelled the slate dump, or "gob pile," near our home. The com-
> pany moved coal-mine waste and slate to the dump all day long. As
> slate accumulates with coal, methane gas builds up. Spontaneous
> combustion often ignites the gas, and coal fires smolder for months.
> Unless the wind blew burning coal smoke away from the slate
> dump, gray smoke hung in the sky all the time. We breathed the poi-
> soned air outside and inside our home and never thought about it.

Although antismoke campaigns were waged in some of America's larger cities beginning in the late nineteenth century, the issue received only scant attention in Appalachia's coal towns. Breathing in coal dust and smoke was as much a part of life in a coal town as shopping at the company store.[11]

Decline and Decay

Consolidation's photos enlighten us about relationships that existed at a particular time and in a particular place—relationships between miners and management; between humans and the physical environment; between Appalachia and the world beyond. To truly appreciate their value, however, it is necessary to see past their visual content. In this book I have argued that the photographs in the Smithsonian Institution collection must be treated not as neutral transcribers of fact, but as texts containing the values, beliefs, and priorities of the company. Delivered to employees via the pages of the company magazine, as well as by other means, the company "message" was effectively disseminated to a wide audience. That company officials would have used photographs in this manner is, of course, not surprising. Governments and businesses have used photographs to "manufacture consent" almost since their inception.[12]

Returning to Jenkinjones, West Virginia—a company town owned by the Pocahontas Fuel Company—Jack Owens found much to remind him of his childhood even though more than thirty years had passed since he left town in the late 1960s. Although the old company store and payroll office were falling apart, the United Methodist Church he grew up attending and several other structures remained intact—a "link with the past" he found comforting. Missing were the familiar sounds and voices he had grown accustomed to hearing: "The quiet struck me. The sounds I'd grown up with in the 1940s and 1950s were gone: miners walking up the hollow to the #6 mine, trains pulling in and out of the tipple, cars going to the Company Store, women calling to one another and to their children over backyard clotheslines." While the emphasis of this book has been placed on early twentieth-century photographs, images of company towns taken in the late twentieth century are valuable as well, for they show us the extent to which the built environment we have seen represented in the Consol collection has both survived and decayed over time, not to mention the degree to which the coal industry in Appalachia has both survived and decayed. Ironically, they also represent a reversal of sorts, for now these landscapes are represented and interpreted in ways the company could never have anticipated.[13]

Notes

Introduction

1. Smithsonian Institution, National Museum of American History, "A Guide to the Collection: The Pittsburgh Consolidation Coal Company Records, Consolidation Coal Company Photographs," 13 January 1998 (draft).

2. William Cronon, "Comment: Cutting Loose or Running Aground," *Journal of American History* 20 (1): 38–43; David Lowenthal, *The Past Is a Foreign Country* (Cambridge: Cambridge University Press, 1985), 191, 235; Cole Harris, "The Historical Mind and the Practice of Geography," in *Humanistic Geography: Prospects and Problems,* ed. David Ley and Marwyn S. Samuels (London: Croom Helm, 1978), 131.

3. Peirce F. Lewis, "Axioms for Reading the Landscape: Some Guides to the American Scene," in *The Interpretation of Ordinary Landscapes: Geographical Essays,* ed. Donald W. Meinig (New York: Oxford University Press, 1979), 25.

4. Richard V. Francaviglia, "Mining and Landscape Transformation," in *The American Environment: Interpretations of Past Geographies,* ed. Lary M. Dilsaver and Craig E. Colten (Lanham, Md.: Rowman & Littlefield, 1992), 92. For an examination of the controversy revolving around mountaintop removal, see Jeff Goodell, "How Coal Got Its Glow Back," *New York Times Magazine,* 22 July 2001, 30–37, 44, 62–63; and Rudy Abramson, "Mountaintop Removal: Necessity or Nightmare?" *Now and Then,* Winter 2001, 20–24; and Jedediah S. Purdy, "Rape of the Appalachians," in *Appalachia: Social Context Past and Present,* ed. Phillip J. Obermiller and Michael E. Maloney (Dubuque: Kendall/Hunt Publishing, 2002), 208–14.

5. Crandall A. Shifflett, *Coal Towns: Life, Work, and Culture in Company Towns of Southern Appalachia, 1880–1960* (Knoxville: University of Tennessee Press, 1991), 27, 29; A. J. Christiansen, *Production of Coal: Bituminous and Anthracite, Years 1800 to 1947 by States and Producing Districts and the United States* (Chicago: Northern Illinois Coal Trade Association, 1948); Duane A. Smith, *Mining America: The Industry and the Environment, 1800–1980* (Niwot, Colo.: University Press of Colorado, 1993), 2. Richard V. Francaviglia states: "The railroads constructed to get mineral products to more distant urban markets underscore the isolation of mining districts. In fact, it can be argued that most of the major coal and metals mining districts could never have developed without their railways, many of which were constructed by the same outside investors who capitalized the mines. The relationship between mining and railroading is intimate and is seen everywhere in the landscape." Francaviglia,

Hard Places: Reading the Landscape of America's Historic Mining Districts (Iowa City: University of Iowa Press, 1991), 73.

6. Margaret M. Mulrooney, "A Legacy of Coal: The Coal Company Towns of Southwestern Pennsylvania," in *Perspectives in Vernacular Architecture,* IV, ed. Thomas Carter and Bernard L. Herman (Columbia: University of Missouri, 1991), 130; Francaviglia, *Hard Places,* 195.

7. Brian Black, "Petrolia: A Sacrificial Landscape of American Industrialization," *Landscape* 32 (2) (1994): 42–48.

8. John C. Hennen, *The Americanization of West Virginia: Creating a Modern Industrial State, 1916–1925* (Lexington: University Press of Kentucky, 1996), 102.

9. William Graebner, *Coal-Mining Safety in the Progressive Period: The Political Economy of Reform* (Lexington: University Press of Kentucky, 1976), 9.

10. Catherine A. Lutz and Jane L. Collins, *Reading* National Geographic (Chicago: University of Chicago Press, 1993); Joan M. Schwartz, "'We Make Our Tools and Our Tools Make Us': Lessons from Photographs for the Practice, Politics, and Poetics of Diplomatics," *Archivaria* 40 (Fall 1995): 42; John Berger, "Understanding the Photograph," in *Classic Essays on Photography,* ed. Alan Trachtenberg (New Haven: Leete's Island Books, 1980), 292, italics in original.

11. Schwartz, "'We Make Our Tools,'" 44, 48.

12. Allen W. Batteau, *The Invention of Appalachia* (Tucson: University of Arizona Press, 1990), 84. In this chapter I have relied on the following company-generated or sponsored histories: William Jasper Nicolls, *Above Ground and Below in the George's Creek Coal Region* (Baltimore: Consolidation Coal Company, 1898); C. L. Green, "The Consolidation Coal Company," *CCC Mutual Monthly,* September–October 1926, 19–26; Charles E. Beachley, *History of the Consolidation Coal Company, 1864–1934* (New York: Consolidation Coal Company, 1934); George H. Love, *An Exciting Century in Coal, 1864–1964,* address given by the president of the Pittsburgh Consolidation Coal Company at Pittsburgh (New York: Newcomen Society in North America, 1955); Consolidation Coal Company, *A History of Consolidation Coal Company* (Pittsburgh: Consolidation Coal Company, Public Relations Department, 1989), 2.

13. Smith, *Mining America,* 168.

Chapter 1

1. See, for example, Susan Sontag, "Looking At War: Photography's View of Devastation and Death," *New Yorker,* 9 December 2002.

2. Yi Fu Tuan, "Sight and Pictures," *Geographical Review* 69 (October 1979): 413–22.

3. Donald W. Meinig, "The Beholding Eye: Ten Versions of the Same Scene," in *The Interpretation of Ordinary Landscapes: Geographical Essays,* ed. Donald W. Meinig (New York: Oxford University Press, 1979), 34; Yi-Fu Tuan, "Thought and Landscape: The Eye and the Mind's Eye," in Meinig, *Ordinary Landscapes,* 89–102; P. Lewis, "Reading the Landscape," 23, italics in original; Denis Cosgrove, *Social Formation and Symbolic Landscape* (London: Croom Helm, 1984), 9. See also Peirce Lewis, "The Monument and the Bungalow," *Geographical Review* 88 (October 1998): 507–27.

4. Toni Alexander, "The Deceptive Landscape: A Study in Ethnicity in Hornitos, California, 1860–1900," *California Geographer* 42 (2002): 41–59; Cosgrove, *Social Formation,* 13; Denis Cosgrove, "Prospect, Perspective, and the Evolution of the Landscape Idea," in *Reading Human Geography: The Poetics and Politics of Inquiry,* ed. Trevor Barnes and Derek Gregory (London: Arnold, 1997); Denis Cosgrove and Stephen Daniels, eds., *The Iconography of Landscape: Essays on the Symbolic Representation, Design and Use of Past Environments* (Cambridge: Cambridge University Press, 1988); James Duncan and Nancy Duncan, "(Re)reading the Landscape," *Environment and Planning D: Society and Space* 6 (1988): 117–26; Deryck W. Holdsworth, "Landscape and Archives as Texts," in *Understanding Ordinary Landscapes,* ed. Paul Groth and Todd W. Bressi (New Haven: Yale University Press, 1997), 44; Edward Relph, *Rational Landscapes and Humanistic Geography* (London: Croom Helm, 1981); Richard H. Schein, "The Place of Landscape: A Conceptual Framework for Interpreting an American Scene," *Annals of the Association of American Geographers* 87 (4) (1997): 660–80; Bret Wallach, *At Odds with Progress* (Tucson: University of Arizona Press, 1991), viii. For a thorough and highly readable review of cultural geography and the landscape concept, see Don Mitchell, *Cultural Geography: A Critical Introduction* (Oxford: Blackwell Publishers, 2000). James and Nancy Duncan's statement regarding the treatment of landscapes as texts is particularly relevant: "If landscapes are texts which are read, interpreted according to an ingrained cultural framework of interpretation, if they are often read 'inattentively' at a practical or nondiscursive level, then they may be inculcating their readers with a set of notions about how the society is organized: and their readers may be largely unaware of this" ("(Re)reading the Landscape," 123).

5. J. B. Harley, "Maps, Knowledge, and Power," in *The Iconography of Landscape: Essays on the Symbolic Representation, Design and Use of Past Environments,* ed. Denis Cosgrove and Stephen Daniels (Cambridge: Cambridge University Press, 1988), 278, 282, 290, 303; Matthew H. Edney, *Mapping an Empire: The Geographical Construction of British India, 1765–1843* (Chicago: University of Chicago Press, 1997); Carolyn Merchant, *The Columbia Guide to American Environmental History* (New York: Columbia University Press, 2002).

6. John W. Reps, *Cities on Stone: Nineteenth Century Lithograph Images of the Urban West* (Fort Worth: Amon Carter Museum, 1976), 7; John W. Reps, *Bird's Eye Views: Historic Lithographs of North American Cities* (New York: Princeton Architectural Press, 1998).

7. R. H. Schein, "Representing Urban America: Nineteenth-Century Views of Landscape, Space, and Power," *Environment and Planning D: Society and Space* 11 (1993): 8–10, 17–19. As Reps points out, some scenes even showed buildings and railroad lines that had yet to be constructed, a sure sign that they were utilized by railroad officials and local boosters to lure investors and encourage future settlement and growth (Reps, *Cities on Stone*).

8. Mary Warner Marien, *Photography and Its Critics: A Cultural History, 1839–1900* (Cambridge: Cambridge University Press, 1993); David E. Nye, *Image Worlds: Corporate Identities at General Electric, 1890–1930* (Cambridge, Mass.: MIT Press, 1985); Alan Trachtenberg, *Reading American Photographs: Images as History,*

Mathew Brady to Walker Evans (New York: Hill and Wang, 1989); Joan M. Schwartz, "*The Geography Lesson:* Photographs and the Construction of Imaginative Geographies," *Journal of Historical Geography* 22 (1) (1996): 16–45.

9. Steven Hoelscher, "The Photographic Construction of Tourist Space in Victorian America," *Geographical Review* 88 (October 1998): 548–70; Schwartz, "*Geography Lesson,*" 33; Allan Sekula, "Photography between Labour and Capital," in *Mining Photographs and Other Pictures: A Selection from the Negative Archives of Shedden Studio, Glace Bay, Cape Breton, 1948–1968,* ed. Benjamin H. D. Buchloh and Robert Wilkie (Halifax: Press of the Nova Scotia College of Art and Design, 1983), 193. Hoelscher also argues that geographers have not examined photographs as thoroughly as have members of other disciplines: "Critical readings of landscape representations have become standard fare for cultural geographers in recent years. Nuanced and provocative work by scholars on both sides of the Atlantic have demonstrated the importance of landscape imagery for the historical-geographical interpretation of social ideologies, of individual meaning, and of the complex web of power relations. But while analyses of literary texts, paintings, and garden designs have established the fruitfulness of the iconographic approach to landscape, photography has remained curiously peripheral." Scholars in cognate fields have been less reluctant to utilize photographs for more than simple illustrative purposes ("Photographic Construction," 548).

10. Tuan, "Sight and Pictures"; Schwartz, "'We Make Our Tools,'" 47.

11. William Wyckoff and Lary M. Dilsaver, "Promotional Imagery of Glacier National Park," *Geographical Review* 87 (January 1997): 1–26.

12. Schwartz, "*Geography Lesson,*" 29; Hoelscher, "Photographic Construction," 565. See also Joan M. Schwartz, "'Records of Simple Truth and Precision': Photography, Archives, and the Illusion of Control," *Archivaria* 50 (Fall 2000): 1–40.

13. Lutz and Collins, *Reading National Geographic,* 12, 82; Fred Ritchin, *In Our Own Image: The Coming Revolution in Photography* (New York: Aperture, 1990).

14. Nye, *Image Worlds,* 149; Jon M. Williams and Daniel T. Muir, *Corporate Images: Photography and the DuPont Company, 1865–1972* (Wilmington, Del.: Hagley Museum and Library, 1984), 27; Sekula, "Photography between Labour and Capital," 234.

15. Brian Black, "Recasting the Unalterable Order of Nature: Photography and the First Oil Boom," *Pennsylvania History: A Journal of Mid-Atlantic Studies* 64 (Spring 1997), 277–78. See also Walter Rundell Jr., *Early Texas Oil* (College Station: Texas A&M University Press, 1977).

16. Robert E. Snyder, "Photography and the American South: A Bibliographical Introduction," *History of Photography* 19 (Spring 1995): 1–3, 1; Jerry Bruce Thomas, *An Appalachian New Deal: West Virginia in the Great Depression* (Lexington: University Press of Kentucky, 1998). There are a number of sources that provide valuable introductions to the work of Farm Security Administration photographers. These include Beverly W. Brannan and David Horvath, eds., *A Kentucky Album: Farm Security Administration Photographs, 1935–1943* (Lexington: University Press of Kentucky, 1986); Andrea Fisher, *Let Us Now Praise Famous Women: Women Photographers for the U.S. Government, 1935 to 1944* (London: Pandora, 1987); Carl Fleischhauer and Beverly W. Brannan, eds., *Documenting America, 1935–1943, with Essays by Lawrence W. Levine and Alan Trachtenberg* (Berkeley: University of California Press, in associa-

tion with Library of Congress, 1988); Brooks Johnson, ed., *Mountaineers to Main Streets: The Old Dominion Seen through the Farm Security Administration Photographs* (Norfolk: Chrysler Museum, 1985); Martha Rosler, "In, Around, and Afterthoughts (on Documentary Photography)," in *The Context of Meaning: Critical Histories of Photography* (Cambridge, Mass.: MIT Press, 1989); Maren Stange, "Documentary Photography in American Social Reform: The FSA Project and Its Predecessors," in *Multiple Views: Logan Grant Essays on Photography, 1983–1989,* ed. Daniel P. Younger (Albuquerque: University of New Mexico Press, 1991); Margaret R. Weiss, *Ben Shahn, Photographer: An Album from the Thirties* (New York: Da Capo Press, 1973). See also John R. Kemp, ed., *Lewis Hine: Photographs of Child Labor in the New South* (Jackson, Miss.: University Press of Mississippi, 1986).

17. Schwartz, "'We Make Our Tools'"; Schwartz, "*Geography Lesson,*" 35; F. Jack Hurley, "The Farm Security Administration File: In and Out of Focus," *History of Photography* 17 (Autumn 1993): 244.

18. Melissa A. McEuen, "Doris Ulmann and Marion Post Wolcott: The Appalachian South," *History of Photography* 19 (Spring 1995): 4–12; Susan H. Edwards, "Ben Shahn: The Road South," *History of Photography* 19 (Spring 1995): 13–19.

19. Hurley, "Farm Security Administration," 246; Alan Trachtenberg, "From Image to Story: Reading the File," in *Documenting America, 1935–1943,* ed. Carl Fleischhauer and Beverly W. Brannan (Berkeley: University of California Press, in association with the Library of Congress, 1988), 43–73. Lutz and Collins point out that the magazine's editors provide their photographers with themes to "focus the photographer" and to "organize the picture-taking enterprise" (*Reading* National Geographic, 55). They add that posed shots have also been used.

20. Edwards, "Ben Shahn," 13, 16. That FSA photographers had a lasting impact that carried well into the late twentieth century is revealed by Lutz and Collins: "In discussing the truth status of the work they produce, *National Geographic* photographers often relate their work to the tradition of documentary photography, particularly to the photographic work sponsored by the Farm Security Administration in the 1930s and 1940s. These are 'deep' photographs that speak to the human condition, but they are also popularly held to be factual in content" (*Reading* National Geographic, 63).

21. McEuen, "Doris Ulmann," 4–6.

22. Nye, *Image Worlds,* 9; Schwartz, "'We Make Our Tools'"; Mona Domosh, "Visual Texts in Historical Geography," *Historical Geography* 29 (2001): 68.

23. Black, "Order of Nature," 283.

24. Schwartz, "*Geography Lesson,*" 34, italics in original; Holdsworth, "Landscape and Archives," 44; Schwartz, "'Simple Truth and Precision.'"

25. Geoffrey L. Buckley and Timothy G. Anderson, "The Consolidation Coal Company Photograph Collection, 1910–1945," *Appalachian Journal: A Regional Studies Review* 27 (Fall 1999): 62–83.

26. Geoffrey L. Buckley and Betsy Burstein, "When Coal Was King: The Consolidation Coal Company's Maryland Division Photographs," *Maryland Historical Magazine* 91 (Fall 1996): 298–310. According to the National Museum of American History's *Guide to the Collection,* the Consolidation Coal Company photographs are divided into four groups or series: Negatives; Original Prints; Miscellaneous Resources;

and Miscellaneous Material. The first series is subdivided into three subseries. The first, Kentucky Negatives, consists of over fifteen hundred glass plate and film negatives numbered from CCC1 to CCC3707. The fact that the total number of negatives and the numbering system do not match indicates that many negatives are missing from the collection. The second subseries contains approximately two hundred forty unnumbered glass plate negatives plus a few film negatives. The third subseries is made up of two boxes of copy negatives. According to museum authorities, these may be copies of original prints in subseries 2a, for which there are no original negatives. The second series comprises original prints, many of which were produced from the negatives in series 1. The photos in this series have been divided into nine separate subseries. The first, subseries 2a, was produced from negatives in subseries 1a. These prints, 1,372 in all, focus on the company's operations in Kentucky and are arranged chronologically in nineteen binders. Many of the photos are accompanied by typewritten captions and may once have been mounted in company albums. The photographs are silver-gelatin prints on matte paper. Many have been dry-mounted to black or gray construction paper, or are mounted back-to-back. Subseries 2b contains twenty company albums and one booklet of photographs. Eighteen of the albums are bound with black leather, with pages held together by heavy string. They are embossed with gold lettering, organized geographically, and titled according to company division (e.g., Elkhorn Division). While most of the pictures are from Kentucky and West Virginia., one album features scenes from the Maryland and Pennsylvania divisions. Most of the Kentucky prints are duplicates from subseries 2a. Subseries 2c, the J. E. Brown prints, includes some five hundred photographs believed to have been produced by the J. E. Brown studio of Stamford, Connecticut. They are numbered 1–722, indicating that many are missing. Subseries 2d, West Virginia Prints, contains original photographs of Fairmont Coal and Consolidation Coal company towns in West Virginia, machines of the Fairmont Mining Machinery Company, and trolleys of the Fairmont and Clarksburg Traction Company. The majority of these photos appear to have been removed from albums similar to those in other parts of the collection. Subseries 2e, Miscellaneous Original Prints, consists of one binder of unidentified original photos from Kentucky and West Virginia mining towns. Subseries 2f, Miscellaneous Kentucky Prints, is made up of a single binder of photographs of Kentucky mining towns. It is likely that these were once mounted in company albums. Subseries 2g, Mineral Fuel Company Prints, is a binder of fifty-eight photographs showing the activities of the Mineral Fuel Company of Fleming, Kentucky. Subseries 2h, Portraits, is a collection of formal portraits of company personnel, including salesmen, directors, presidents, and other officials. The single binder of images is organized by rank of employee and office location. Subseries 2i, Miscellaneous Oversize Prints, is contained in a single box and was likely part of another subseries at one time. Images are of West Virginia mining towns, the Fairmont and Clarksburg Traction Company, the Fairmont Coal Company, the Mineral Fuel Company, plus four pictures of a CCC exhibition in a foreign country. Series 3 and 4 contain supporting documents pertaining to either the collection or the Consolidation Coal Company.

27. According to Lanna and Charles Dixon of Jenkins, Kentucky, Consol had a company photographer on their payroll named Charlie Morgan. The company also

had a photo lab where these pictures were developed. When Beth-Elkhorn took over from Consol, they also had a company photographer. Wyckoff and Dilsaver report that many of the photographs in the Great Northern collection were kept in scrapbooks "sent periodically to company superiors for inspection" ("Promotional Imagery," 7).

28. Hennen, *Americanization of West Virginia,* 102–3.

29. Stephen P. Hanna, "Representation and the Reproduction of Appalachian Space: A History of Contested Signs and Meanings," *Historical Geography* 28 (2000): 179–207.

Chapter 2

1. Harry M. Caudill, *Theirs Be the Power: The Moguls of Eastern Kentucky* (Urbana: University of Illinois Press, 1983), 5, 36; Shifflett, *Coal Towns,* 29.

2. Geoffrey L. Buckley, "Converting Minerals into Merchandise: Landownership and Environmental Alteration in the George's Creek Valley of Western Maryland, 1789–1842," *Historical Geography* 26 (1998): 151–75. For a treatment of the early history of the Baltimore and Ohio Railroad, see James D. Dilts, *The Great Road: The Building of the Baltimore and Ohio, the Nation's First Railroad, 1828–1853* (Stanford: Stanford University Press, 1993); Milton Reizenstein, *The Economic History of the Baltimore and Ohio Railroad, 1827–1853* (Baltimore: Johns Hopkins Press, 1897). See also John F. Stover, *History of the Baltimore and Ohio Railroad* (West Lafayette, Ind.: Purdue University Press, 1987).

3. William Bullock Clark, *Maryland Geological Survey: Report on the Coals of Maryland* (Baltimore: Johns Hopkins Press, 1905); "The Coal Field of Allegany County, Maryland," *National Magazine and Industrial Record* 1 (October 1845): 431–43; Charles Lyell, *Travels in North America: With Geological Observations on the United States, Canada, and Nova Scotia* (London: J. Murray, 1845), 14; J. Thomas Scharf, *History of Western Maryland* (1882; reprint, Baltimore: Regional Publishing Company, 1968), 1438. For more on the region's history during this period, see also Katherine A. Harvey, *The Best-Dressed Miners: Life and Labor in the Maryland Coal Region, 1835–1910* (Ithaca: Cornell University Press, 1969); G. E. Kershaw, "Allegany County: The Frontier Years," in *Allegany County, A History* (Parsons, W.Va.: McClain Printing Company, 1976).

4. *Cumberland Sunday Times,* 13 April 1947; K. Harvey, *Best-Dressed Miners;* W. B. Robbins, *Cheap Fuel* (Louisville: Kentucky Fuel Company, 1 November 1855), 1, italics in original.

5. Donna M. Ware, "Rails, Resources, and Resorts: The Opening of Maryland's Coal Region," *Maryland Humanities* (Spring/Summer 1995): 11–13; David Mushet, Analysis of the coal and iron ores in England: Extracts of a Letter from David Mushet, Esq., to Samuel Swartwout, Esq., 20 September 1838; Benjamin Silliman, *Extracts from a report made to the Maryland Mining Company on the estate of said company, in the county of Allegany, Maryland* (New York: Printed by Scatcherd and Adams, 1838), 8, 20; Benjamin Silliman, *Extracts from a report made to the Maryland and New York Coal & Iron Company on the estate of said company, in the county of Alleghany [sic], state of Maryland* (London: Printed by T. C. Savill, 1839), 23; See also

Donna M. Ware, *Green Glades and Sooty Gob Piles: The Maryland Coal Region's Industrial and Architectural Past* (Crownsville: Maryland Historical and Cultural Publications, 1995).

6. George W. Hughes, *Excerpts From Reports of an Examination of the Coal Measures Belonging to the Maryland Mining Company in Allegany County and of a Survey for a Railroad from The Mines to the Chesapeake and Ohio Canal, at Cumberland* (Washington, D.C.: Printed by Gales and Seaton, 1837), 16–17; Henry Thomas Weld to John Wright, Esq., 1838 (copy on file at the University of Maryland, McKeldin Library); "Coal Field of Allegany County."

7. D. M. Dean, "New Directions, 1800–1865," in *Allegany County, A History* (Parsons, W.Va.: McClain Printing Company, 1976), 91–199; Ware, "Rails, Resources, and Resorts"; K. C. Lacoste and R. D. Wall, *An Archaeological Study of the Western Maryland Coal Region: The Historic Resources* (Baltimore: Maryland Geological Survey, 1987). For the location of squatter tracts in Allegany County, see "Map of Military Lots, Tracts, Escheats, &c. in Garrett County, MD and Allegany County, MD West of Cumberland. Prepared Under Act of 1874 Chapter 322 &c. Scale: 200 Perches to 1 Inch" (copy on file at Maryland State Archives, Annapolis). For a detailed examination of landownership change in the George's Creek valley, see Buckley, "Minerals into Merchandise." The literature on land speculation in Appalachia is extensive. I found the following sources particularly valuable: Ray A. Billington, "The Origin of the Speculator as a Frontier Type," *Agricultural History* 19 (October 1945): 204–12; Wilma Dunaway, *The First American Frontier: Transition to Capitalism in Southern Appalachia, 1700–1860* (Chapel Hill: University of North Carolina Press, 1996); Ronald D. Eller, *Miners, Millhands, and Mountaineers: Industrialization of the Appalachian South, 1880–1930* (Knoxville: University of Tennessee Press, 1982); Aubrey C. Land, "A Land Speculator in the Opening of Western Maryland," *Maryland Historical Magazine* 48 (3) (1953): 191–203; Ronald L. Lewis, "Appalachian Restructuring in Historical Perspective: Coal, Culture and Social Change in West Virginia," *Urban Studies* 30 (2) (1993): 299–308; Robert D. Mitchell, *Commercialism and Frontier: Perspectives on the Early Shenandoah Valley* (Charlottesville: University Press of Virginia, 1977); Barbara Rasmussen, *Absentee Landownership and Exploitation in West Virginia, 1760–1920* (Lexington: University of Kentucky Press, 1994).

8. Beachley, *Consolidation Coal Company*, 15–16; Deane Mellander, *The Cumberland and Pennsylvania Railroad: Western Maryland's Historic Coal Carrier* (Newton, N.J.: Carstens Publications, 1981), 6; *Cumberland Alleganian*, 6 March 1846, 8 May 1847; *CCC Mutual Monthly*, May–June 1928, 3. Charles Beachley was, incidentally, secretary and assistant treasurer of the Consolidation Coal Company.

9. Beachley, *Consolidation Coal Company*, 9.

10. Katherine A. Harvey, "Building a Frontier Iron Works: Problems of Transport and Supply, 1837–1840," *Maryland Historical Magazine* 70 (Summer 1975), 149–66; Beachley, *Consolidation Coal Company;* Mellander, *Cumberland and Pennsylvania Railroad;* "Coal Field of Allegany County," 442; *Cumberland Alleganian*, 28 August, 13 November 1847; John Lauritz Larson, *Bonds of Enterprise: John Murray Forbes and Western Development in America's Railway Age* (Boston: Harvard University Press, 1984), 21.

11. Allan Nevins and Henry Steele Commager, *A Short History of the United States* (New York: Random House, 1945), 257, 259, 301; Smith, *Mining America*, 52.

12. Ware, "Rails, Resources, and Resorts"; Geoffrey L. Buckley, "The Environmental Transformation of an Appalachian Valley, 1850–1906," *Geographical Review* 88 (April 1998): 175–98; Love, *Exciting Century*, 9; Nevins and Commager, *History of the United States*. For a concise and fascinating examination of the persistence of absentee landownership and its effects in southern Appalachia, see John Gaventa, "The Political Economy of Land Tenure: Appalachia and the Southeast," in *Who Owns America? Social Conflict over Property Rights*, ed. Harvey M. Jacobs (Madison: University of Wisconsin Press, 1998), 227–44.

13. *Cumberland Union and Allegany County Gazette*, 30 September 1865; K. Harvey, *Best-Dressed Miners*, 10. Alarmed that the economic panic of 1873 might precipitate a revolt against outside interests in the coal fields of western Maryland and disrupt business, Beachley notes that some of the directors of the Consolidation Coal Company suggested a preventive measure: "On February 6, 1875, a meeting of Consolidation stockholders was held in New York and the situation discussed at length. There were some who strongly advocated the removal of the Company's offices to Cumberland or Mount Savage, believing that such a move would allay local prejudice against 'outside capitalists.' Resolutions authorizing the move were introduced only to be voted down in a fight so bitter that the stockholders ended by turning out those directors who voted for the resolutions and filling their places with new men. The office remained in New York" (Beachley, *Consolidation Coal Company*, 24). John B. Wiseman offers, "Responding to local fears of alien corporate power, Consolidation moved its headquarters from New York City to Baltimore in 1877." Wiseman, "The Whirligig of Change, 1865–1920," in *Allegany County, A History* (Parsons, W.Va.: McClain Printing Company, 1976), 208.

14. Beachley, *Consolidation Coal Company*, 17, 19. According to Scharf, although the Consolidation Coal Company was chartered in 1860 its organization was delayed by the Civil War.

15. Letter in Beachley, *Consolidation Coal Company*, 20; *Cumberland Alleganian*, 26 January 1870.

16. *Cumberland Alleganian*, 16 February, italics in original; 2, 30 March 1870; Beachley, *Consolidation Coal Company*, 21; Scharf, *History of Western Maryland*.

17. Beachley, *Consolidation Coal Company*.

18. Caudill, *Theirs Be the Power*, 42; Geoffrey C. Ward, *Before the Trumpet: Young Franklin Roosevelt, 1882–1905* (New York: Harper and Row, 1985).

19. Beachley, *Consolidation Coal Company*, 24; Wiseman, "Whirligig of Change," 205.

20. *Cumberland Alleganian*, 29 February 1904; Scharf, *History of Western Maryland*, 1443.

21. Beachley, *Consolidation Coal Company*, 51; K. Harvey, *Best-Dressed Miners*.

22. Scharf, *History of Western Maryland*, 1444.

23. *Cumberland Daily Times*, 4 June 1885, 11 August 1886; *Cumberland Alleganian*, 7 March 1866, 17 July, 24 August, 6 November 1899, 15 January, 15 March 1900, 2 January 1903, 22 December 1904, 2 November 1905; Ronald L. Lewis, *Transforming the Appalachian Countryside: Railroads, Deforestation, and Social Change in West Virginia, 1880–1920* (Chapel Hill: University of North Carolina Press, 1998); Love, *Exciting Century*, 10.

24. Love, *Exciting Century*, 11; Eller, *Miners, Millhands, and Mountaineers*.

25. Green, "Consolidation Coal Company"; Richard B. Drake, *A History of Appalachia* (Lexington: University Press of Kentucky, 2001); John Alexander Williams, *West Virginia and the Captains of Industry* (Morgantown: West Virginia University Foundation, 1976); H. A. Williamson, "A Comprehensive Survey of the Fairmont Region: The geographical location of a great coal field, the nature of the surface and coal seams—the railroads that serve it, and its commercial history," reprinted from the *Coal and Coal Trade Journal*, *CCC Mutual Monthly*, May–June 1927, 8–12; Beachley, *Consolidation Coal Company.*

26. Ewing G. Wells, "Millers Creek Division Traces Its Development to Company Formed in 1847," *CCC Mutual Monthly*, May–June 1928, 30; *CCC Mutual Monthly*, May–June 1928, 3; Elizabeth W. Dramcyzk, *The History of Jenkins, Kentucky, Compiled in Honor of the Sixtieth Anniversary Homecoming Celebration, 1912–1973*, sponsored by Jenkins Area Jaycees.

27. Caudill, *Theirs Be the Power;* Drake, *History of Appalachia;* R. Lewis, *Transforming the Appalachian Countryside,* 62; Eller, *Miners, Millhands, and Mountaineers;* David Alan Corbin, *Life, Work, and Rebellion in the Coal Fields: The Southern West Virginia Miners, 1880–1922* (Urbana: University of Illinois Press, 1981); Williams, *Captains of Industry; CCC Mutual Monthly,* July 1918, 18.

28. Green, "Consolidation Coal Company"; Love, *Exciting Century,* 12.

29. Green, "Consolidation Coal Company."

30. Timothy Collins, Ronald D. Eller, and Glen Edward Taul, *Kentucky River Area Development District: Historical Trends and Geographic Patterns* (Lexington: University of Kentucky, Appalachian Center, 1996), 7; Love, *Exciting Century,* 14; Consolidation Coal Company, *History,* 6. For a sobering account of the impact of the Great Depression on the coal industry in central Appalachia, see Thomas, *Appalachian New Deal.*

31. Smith, *Mining America,* 123; Love, *Exciting Century,* 15; Consolidation Coal Company, *History,* 6–7. *Pittsburgh* was dropped from the company's name in 1958.

32. Caudill, *Theirs Be the Power.*

Chapter 3

1. Jack E. Weller, *Yesterday's People: Life in Contemporary Appalachia* (Lexington: University Press of Kentucky, 1965), 87; David H. Mould, "The Company Town That Outlived the Company: Haydenville, Ohio," *Journal of Cultural Geography* 5 (Spring/Summer 1985), 71. Compare Weller's description of rural Appalachia with that of William Least Heat-Moon: "In the distance rose the foothills of the Appalachians, old mountains that once separated the Atlantic from the shallow inland sea now the middle of America. The licks came out of the hills, the fields got smaller, and there were little sawmills cutting hardwoods into pallets, crates, fenceposts. The houses shrank, and their colors changed from white to pastels to iridescents to no paint at all. The lawns went from Vertagreen bluegrass to thin fescue to hard-packed dirt glinting with fragments of glass, and the lawn ornaments changed from birdbaths to plastic flamingoes and donkeys to broken-down automobiles with raised hoods like tombstones. On the porches stood long-legged wringer washers and ruined sofas, and, by the front doors, washtubs hung like coats of arms." Heat-Moon, *Blue Highways: A Journey into America* (Boston: Little, Brown, 1982), 24–25.

2. "The Editor's Impression of Elkhorn Division Stores Opening," *CCC Mutual*

Monthly, May–June 1927, 13. A number of scholars have examined the decline of the coal-mining industry in Appalachia and the various issues involved. They include, but are not limited to: Drake, *History of Appalachia;* Paul Salstrom, *Appalachia's Path to Dependency: Rethinking a Region's Economic History,* 1730–1940 (Lexington: University Press of Kentucky, 1994); Thomas, *Appalachian New Deal.*

3. Mould, "Company Town," 72; Crandall Shifflett, "Coaltowns: The Company Town and Southern Appalachian History," in *Appalachia: Social Context Past and Present,* ed. Bruce Ergood and Bruce E. Kuhre, 3d ed. (Dubuque: Kendall/Hunt Publishing, 1991); Jack Temple Kirby, *Rural Worlds Lost: The American South, 1920–1960* (Baton Rouge: Louisiana State University Press, 1987); Drake, *History of Appalachia,* 145–46; Corbin, *Life, Work, and Rebellion,* 8; Richard Melzer, "A Death in Dawson: The Demise of a Southwestern Company Town," *New Mexico Historical Review* 55 (4) (1980): 309–30. On this last point, Melzer reports that in 1950 four out of every five miners in the U.S. "had either purchased homes or were now renting from private landlords rather than from their employers" (310).

4. James B. Allen, *The Company Town in the American West* (Norman: University of Oklahoma Press, 1966), 1; Weller, *Yesterday's People,* 92–93; See also Alan Banks, "Class Formation in the Southeastern Kentucky Coalfields, 1890–1920," in *Appalachia in the Making: The Mountain South in the Nineteenth Century,* ed. Mary Beth Pudup, Dwight B. Billings, and Altina L. Waller (Chapel Hill: University of North Carolina Press, 1995), 321–46; Batteau, *Invention of Appalachia;* Eller, *Miners, Millhands, and Mountaineers,* 162; Francaviglia, *Hard Places;* John Gaventa, *Power and Powerlessness, Quiescence and Rebellion in an Appalachian Valley* (Urbana: University of Illinois Press, 1980); Shifflett, *Coal Towns;* Corbin, *Life, Work, and Rebellion;* Thomas, *Appalachian New Deal.* For an example of the restrictive nature of company rules, see Katherine A. Harvey, ed., "The Lonaconing Journals: The Founding of a Coal and Iron Community, 1837–1840," *Transactions of the American Philosophical Society* 67, pt. 2 (Philadelphia: American Philosophical Society, 1977). For information on company-owned towns located outside the Appalachian region, see Arnold R. Alanen, "The 'Locations': Company Communities on Minnesota's Iron Ranges," *Minnesota History* 48 (Fall 1982): 94–107; Allen, *Company Town;* Michael A. Amundson, "Home on the Range No More: The Boom and Bust of a Wyoming Uranium Mining Town, 1957–1988, *Western Historical Quarterly* 26 (4) (1995): 483–505; Melzer, "Death in Dawson"; Carlos A. Schwantes, *Vision and Enterprise: Exploring the History of Phelps Dodge Corporation* (Tucson: University of Arizona Press, 2000).

5. "New Recreation Buildings," *CCC Mutual Monthly,* December–January 1921–22, 6; "Items from Ida May and Carolina, W.Va.," *CCC Mutual Monthly,* June 1918, 47.

6. Willard Rouse Jillson, *The Topography of Kentucky* (Frankfort: Kentucky Geological Survey, 1927), 45; *CCC Mutual Monthly,* November–December 1925, 39; *CCC Mutual Monthly,* July–August 1926, 48; Alanen, "'Locations.'" There are some parallels between company town development in the Upper Midwest and in Appalachia. Writing about town development on Minnesota's Iron Ranges, Arnold R. Alanen developed a typology which included squatters' locations, company locations, and model locations. With respect to the last of these settlement forms Alanen writes: "No more than ten of these settlements existed throughout the entire Lake Superior region, but the mining companies, perceiving them as highly visible examples of benevolent

paternalism, invested rather heavily in such locations. The management of both the company and model locations was quite similar, although the latter were laid out in a more attractive manner, contained higher quality housing, and were intended primarily for supervisory personnel and highly valued employees" (97).

7. *CCC Mutual Monthly,* April 1922, 55; November 1922, 18, 21; September–October 1926, 53; "Great Improvements Planned for Consol Mines of its West Virginia Division," *CCC Mutual Monthly,* September–October 1926, 18; Eller, *Miners, Millhands, and Mountaineers;* Hugh Griffin, "Our Policy as to Sanitation in Towns," *CCC Mutual Monthly,* May–June 1927, 8, 30.

8. Jillson, *Topography of Kentucky,* 45; Eller, *Miners, Millhands, and Mountaineers,* 183; Thomas, *Appalachian New Deal.*

9. Mulrooney, "Legacy of Coal"; Kirby, *Rural Worlds Lost.* On the connection between corporate paternalism and antiunionism, Kirby provides a useful example: "One of the most self-consciously paternalistic of coal operators was Major William P. Tams. Born in Staunton, Virginia, in 1883 and trained as an engineer, Tams began to mine the great Beckley, West Virginia, coal seam in 1908. Southwest of the town of Beckley he built the village of Tams—about two hundred houses, a church and school. Workers were native whites and blacks and immigrants, almost a microcosm of the southern West Virginia coal boom mining population. Like entrepreneurs everywhere else, Tams abominated unions and even reduced his workday to nine hours and increased pay somewhat above union scale to avoid having to share his power with the United Mine Workers" (295–96). Hennen, *Americanization of West Virginia,* 102.

10. Shifflett, "Coaltowns," 196; Banks, "Class Formation," 338.

11. Banks, "Class Formation," 338; Hennen, *Americanization of West Virginia.*

12. Francaviglia, *Hard Places;* Mould, "Company Town"; Mulrooney, "Legacy of Coal"; Shifflett, *Coal Towns.*

13. Mulrooney, "Legacy of Coal," 131; Green, "Consolidation Coal Company," 22.

14. Mulrooney, "Legacy of Coal," 131; Buckley and Anderson, "Consolidation Photograph Collection."

15. *CCC Mutual Monthly,* December–January 1922–23, 45–46; Mulrooney, "Legacy of Coal," 131; Shifflett, "Coaltowns," 195; Corbin, *Life, Work, and Rebellion.*

16. Mulrooney, "Legacy of Coal," 131–32; Beachley, *Consolidation Coal Company,* 61; Francaviglia, *Hard Places,* 16–17.

17. Mulrooney, "Legacy of Coal," 132; Buckley and Anderson, "Consolidation Photograph Collection"; Eller, *Miners, Millhands, and Mountaineers,* 171.

18. Francaviglia, *Hard Places,* 39; Shifflett, *Coal Towns;* Mould, "Company Town."

19. "The Editor's Impression of Elkhorn Division Stores Opening," *CCC Mutual Monthly,* May–June 1927, 14–15.

20. Shifflett, *Coal Towns,* 177–78; F. R. Lyon, "Co-operation Required by the Operating Department from the Sales Department," *CCC Mutual Monthly,* November–December 1926, 17–18. Corbin notes that locating the post office in the company store afforded company officials the opportunity to inspect and scrutinize incoming and outgoing mail. Corbin, *Life, Work, and Rebellion.*

21. Shifflett, *Coal Towns;* Eller, *Miners, Millhands, and Mountaineers,* 188; Francaviglia, *Hard Places.* In addition to prohibiting other commercial retail opera-

tions, Francaviglia notes that mining companies might also forbid the establishment of saloons and houses of prostitution.

22. Shifflett, *Coal Towns*, 180; "Discontinuance of Scrip," *Check Board*, July 1947, 1; Corbin, *Life, Work, and Rebellion*. In defense of paternalism, Jerry Bruce Thomas notes, some have argued that "Requiring workers to receive part of their payment in scrip had been a means of protecting women and children, because lump-sum payments would result in wages going for 'liquor or labor racketeers.'" Thomas, *Appalachian New Deal*, 100.

23. Shifflett, *Coal Towns*.

24. Eller, *Miners, Millhands, and Mountaineers; CCC Mutual Monthly*, January–February 1927, 10; July–August 1927, 9–10; "New General Manager of Stores," *CCC Mutual Monthly*, September–October 1927, 5; F. S. Wilson, "Our Remodeled Stores," *CCC Mutual Monthly*, May–June 1927, 11–12.

25. Shifflett, *Coal Towns*, 188–89.

26. Eller, *Miners, Millhands, and Mountaineers;* Shifflett, *Coal Towns;* Mulrooney, "Legacy of Coal"; Shifflett, "Coaltowns," 195. Shifflett writes that the immigrant town "gradually shrank in importance while the other two grew until the 1920's." After the Second World War, if not earlier, large numbers of black miners also left the coalfields, although for different reasons.

27. Robert Armstead, *Black Days, Black Dust: The Memories of an African American Coal Miner* (Knoxville: University of Tennessee Press, 2002), 18, 30, 31.

28. "Elementary First Aid for the Miner," *CCC Mutual Monthly*, May, June, July 1918; "The Idle Dollar a Bad Servant," *CCC Mutual Monthly*, March 1918, 20; *CCC Mutual Monthly*, April 1921.

29. "Good News for the Children," *CCC Mutual Monthly*, March 1918, 6; *CCC Mutual Monthly*, May 1920, 32–33.

30. Ronald L. Lewis, "From Peasant to Proletarian: The Migration of Southern Blacks to the Central Appalachian Coalfields," *Journal of Southern History* 55 (February 1989): 77–102; R. Lewis, "Appalachian Restructuring"; *CCC Mutual Monthly*, October 1918, 72; September–October 1924, 50. On a recent trip to Jenkins I noted that even the old cemetery was segregated, with "American" whites occupying one area, immigrant whites another, and African Americans a third.

31. Gary Farley and Bill J. Leonard, "Mountain Preachers, Mountain Ministers," in *Christianity in Appalachia: Profiles in Regional Pluralism,* ed. Bill J. Leonard (Knoxville: University of Tennessee Press, 1999), 160–61; *CCC Mutual Monthly,* March–April 1925, 28; January–February, 1926, 19; October 1918, 52.

32. Hennen, *Americanization of West Virginia*, 100; "DIRTY COAL": Loading It Is Plain Dishonesty," *CCC Mutual Monthly*, January–February 1928, 24; Weller, *Yesterday's People*.

33. Hennen, *Americanization of West Virginia*, 101; *CCC Mutual Monthly*, April 1924, 30.

34. "Victory Gardens," *CCC Mutual Monthly*, October 1919, 2; "Gardens," *CCC Mutual Monthly*, October 1919, 7; "Millers Creek Division Prize Winners in Division Garden Contest," *CCC Mutual Monthly*, November 1918, 21; September 1923, 29; *CCC Mutual Monthly*, October 1918, 8; *CCC Mutual Monthly*, November 1921, 12. According to Jerry Bruce Thomas, the Great Depression caused a "back-to-the-land"

movement to form. The profusion of gardens drew the attention of travelers passing through the region. According to Thomas, "The collapse of mining and urban jobs encouraged movement back to the countryside of some who had moved to the coal camps or to a city for work. In the spring of 1932, a traveler in southern West Virginia observed many gardens prepared on the steep hillsides and wondered how it was possible to plant on such precipitous slopes." Thomas, *Appalachian New Deal*, 60. As geographer David Harvey points out, Henry Ford encouraged his workers to combat the effects of the economic depression of the 1930s by planting vegetables. D. Harvey, *The Condition of Postmodernity: An Enquiry into the Origins of Cultural Change* (Oxford: Basil Blackwell, 1989).

35. CCC *Mutual Monthly*, November 1918, 20.

36. "Gardens," CCC *Mutual Monthly*, June 1918, 12; "A Sorry Mess, They All Confess," CCC *Mutual Monthly*, June 1918, 13; CCC *Mutual Monthly*, April 1921, 10; Hennen, *Americanization of West Virginia*, 5; Thomas, *Appalachian New Deal*, 157.

37. "Victory Gardens," CCC *Mutual Monthly*, October 1918, 8; "Gardens," CCC *Mutual Monthly*, March 1918, 12; Alanen, "'Locations,'" 100. Alanen notes that garden planting was also encouraged on Minnesota's Iron Ranges: "The companies . . . made some effort to beautify location landscapes by encouraging residents to improve their yards and to plant gardens. Throughout the locations the employees held contests with prizes for the most attractive gardens and yards; company bulletins published pictures of the winning projects to serve as examples of what could be accomplished by residents who used their free time wisely."

38. "Annual Garden Contest," CCC *Mutual Monthly*, October 1921, 41–42; "Mines Nos. 204–5," CCC *Mutual Monthly*, October 1919, 18–20.

39. "Annual Garden Contest," CCC *Mutual Monthly*, October 1921, 41–42; "Mines Nos. 204–5," CCC *Mutual Monthly*, October 1919, 13; CCC *Mutual Monthly*, March 1921, 47; Sherry Cable, "From Fussin' to Organizing: Individual and Collective Resistance at Yellow Creek," in *Fighting Back in Appalachia: Traditions of Resistance and Change*, ed. Stephen L. Fisher. Philadelphia: Temple University Press, 1993, 69–83. Company towns were often named for key individuals associated with the firm. Owings was probably named for Clarence Watson's wife, Owings being her maiden name. Similarly, Ida May was likely named for Ida May Watson, sister of Clarence W. Watson. CCC *Mutual Monthly*, July 1918, 18.

40. Paul Salstrom and Steve Hollenhorst, "Increasing Dependency and the Touristization Rag," *Appalachian Journal* 21 (Summer 1994): 418; Corbin, *Life, Work, and Rebellion*.

41. "Visiting Nurses in Mining Towns," CCC *Mutual Monthly*, May 1921, 8. Alanen's comments concerning visiting nurses on Minnesota's Iron Ranges are relevant here: "Another form of direct social welfare was the provision of medical services. Though company doctors had long been evident in mining communities, visiting-nurse programs were initiated by several companies in the early 20th century. Nurses . . . attended the sick, gave instructions in personal and domestic hygiene and domestic science, and assisted families with their monetary, marital, and related problems. . . . One nurse stated that neighborhood feuds among nationality groups posed as serious a difficulty as did health problems." Alanen, "'Locations,'" 101–2.

42. CCC *Mutual Monthly*, March 1923, 27, 31, 41; November 1918, 32.

43. "News from Jenkins," *CCC Mutual Monthly,* November–December 1925, 40; May–June 1927, 15.

44. Buckley and Anderson, "Consolidation Photograph Collection"; Banks, "Class Formation," 322.

45. Green, "Consolidation Coal Company," 19–26; Edward Relph, *The Modern Urban Landscape* (Baltimore: Johns Hopkins University Press, 1987); Alanen, "'Locations,'" 98.

46. Harvey, *Condition of Postmodernity.*

Chapter 4

1. For a detailed account of the accident and rescue operation, see Peter J. Boyer, "Rescue at Quecreek: An Accident and Its Consequences," *New Yorker* (18 November 2002): 56–73.

2. "Coal Mining as a Vocation," *CCC Mutual Monthly,* May 1923, 2; Thomas, *Appalachian New Deal;* Ronald L. Lewis, *Black Coal Miners in America: Race, Class, and Community Conflict, 1780–1980* (Lexington: University Press of Kentucky, 1987).

3. Eller, *Miners, Millhands, and Mountaineers,* 171–72; Armstead, *Black Days,* 123–24.

4. Lutz and Collins, *Reading* National Geographic; Williams and Muir, *Corporate Images,* 20.

5. Douglas L. Crowell, *History of the Coal-Mining Industry in Ohio,* Bulletin no. 72 (Columbus: Ohio Department of Natural Resources, Division of Geological Survey, 1995), 86; Francaviglia, *Hard Places,* xix.

6. Nicolls, *Above Ground,* 15–16.

7. *CCC Mutual Monthly,* March–April 1926; May 1920, 37; November–December 1924.

8. *CCC Mutual Monthly,* March 1918; November–December 1925, 24; March–April 1926; September–October 1926, 75. Vols. 1–11 (1962–72) of *Consol News* can be found in the West Virginia Collection at West Virginia University in Morgantown.

9. Keith Dix, *What's a Coal Miner to Do? The Mechanization of Coal Mining* (Pittsburgh: University of Pittsburgh Press, 1988); Doris Drury, *The Accident Records in Coal Mines of the United States: A Study of the Literature with Comparisons of the Records in Other Coal-Producing Countries* (Bloomington: Department of Economics, Indiana University, 1964), 71; "News from Mine No. 26, W. Va.," *CCC Mutual Monthly,* January–February 1926, 23; *CCC Mutual Monthly,* September–October 1926, 59; November–December 1927, 12.

10. Consolidation Coal Company, *History,* 5.

11. K. Harvey, *Best-Dressed Miners,* 42; *CCC Mutual Monthly,* December–January 1923–24; "Cutting and Shearing: Machines Play Important Role in Solving Coal Mining Problems," *CCC Mutual Monthly,* May–June 1928, 15, 17. Doris Drury notes that by the late 1930s electricity in the mines was commonplace and all but the smaller mines had adopted it. Drury, *Accident Records.*

12. Green, "Consolidation Coal Company," 22.

13. *CCC Mutual Monthly,* May–June 1928, 49.

14. Drury, *Accident Records*, 65, 80; Mark Aldrich, "Preventing 'the Needless Peril of the Coal Mine': The Bureau of Mines and the Campaign against Coal Mine Explosions, 1910–1940," *Technology and Culture* (1995): 483–518; Graebner, *Coal-Mining Safety*.

15. Graebner, *Coal-Mining Safety*; Corbin, *Life, Work, and Rebellion*, 10.

16. National Research Council, Committee on Underground Coal Mine Safety, Commission on Engineering and Technical Systems, *Toward Safer Underground Coal Mines* (Washington, D.C.: National Academy Press, 1982), 48–55; Drury, *Accident Records*; Graebner, *Coal-Mining Safety*. See also R. Glenn Ray, "Portal to Portal: My Experience Mining Coal in Ohio," *Appalachian Journal: A Regional Studies Review* 21 (Fall 1993): 24–49.

17. Drury, *Accident Records*; Graebner, *Coal-Mining Safety*.

18. Frank Hass, "The Explosion at Monongah Number Six and Monongah Number Eight Mines of the Fairmont Coal Company, December 6, 1907" (copy on file at the Fairmont State College Library); *New York Times*, 7, 8, 10, 11, 16 December 1907; *Washington Post*, 7, 9, 10, 11, 12, 13, 16 December 1907; *Fairmont Free Press*, 12, 19 December 1907. Aldrich, "Preventing Needless Peril"; Drury, *Accident Records*; Graebner, *Coal-Mining Safety*.

19. Aldrich, "Preventing Needless Peril"; Graebner, *Coal-Mining Safety*.

20. With respect to medical care in the Georges Creek valley of Maryland, Harvey writes, "By 1907 at least one company, the Consolidation Coal Company, had provided an ambulance at its largest mine to carry injured men to their homes." K. Harvey, *Best-Dressed Miners*, 41; Caption for photo featured in *CCC Mutual Monthly*, November 1918, 60; *CCC Mutual Monthly*, July–August 1925, 12.

21. "Bath Houses at Coal Mines," *CCC Mutual Monthly*, May 1921, 9; *CCC Mutual Monthly*, November–December 1925, 29: the caption that accompanied a photo of a new bathhouse read: "White section of Miners' Bath House, Mine No. 251, W. Va."; K. Harvey, *Best-Dressed Miners*, 43.

22. David A. Zegeer, "The Mechanization of Appalachia's Coal Industry: Consolidation Coal and Town of Jenkins Led the Way," *Kentucky Explorer* 16 (9) (2002): 10; Graebner, *Coal-Mining Safety*, 122; K. Harvey, *Best-Dressed Miners*, 41. William Graebner comments on this, "the most traditional and the least productive" of approaches to the mine safety problem: "Some coal-mining companies, usually the largest ones, undertook to improve conditions in their mines, installing safety equipment and training safety foremen and rescue personnel, even when not required by law to do so. They pursued safety activities through a variety of organizations, including local, state, and regional coal-operator associations, the American Mine Safety Association, and the National Safety Council. Yet operators more commonly were circumspect of even the innocuous activities of these organizations, and if the reports of state mine inspectors are reliable, a majority failed to keep their mines in minimally satisfactory condition, frustrated enforcement of safety codes, and cooperated only under duress." Graebner, *Coal-Mining Safety*, 3.

23. "Pennsylvania Contest of Somerset County First Aid Teams," *CCC Mutual Monthly*, November 1918, 18; "Mines No. 210–215, Ky.," *CCC Mutual Monthly*, July–August 1921, 26.

24. "Proud to be a Miner," *United Mine Workers Journal: A Special Bicentennial Issue*, 15 July 1976, 5; "Department of Safety" (column), *CCC Mutual Monthly*, May 1920, 8–9; *CCC Mutual Monthly*, April 1924, 10–11.

25. "Department of Safety," *CCC Mutual Monthly,* October 1918, 24; *CCC Mutual Monthly,* December–January, 1921–1922, 8; February 1924, 12.

26. Corbin, *Life, Work, and Rebellion;* Alan Banks, "Miners Talk Back: Labor Activism in Southeastern Kentucky in 1922," in *Confronting Appalachian Stereotypes: Back Talk from an American Region,* ed. Dwight B. Billings, Gurney Norman, and Katherine Ledford (Lexington: University Press of Kentucky, 1999), 215–27.

27. Hennen, *Americanization of West Virginia;* "Patriotism," *CCC Mutual Monthly,* November 1922, 11; "Whither Go We?" *CCC Mutual Monthly,* March 1923, 1–2; "The Perils of Indifference," *CCC Mutual Monthly,* September 1923. This last article focuses on the threat of communism.

28. Hennen, *Americanization of West Virginia,* 1, 4, 67.

29. Ibid., 2–3; "The American Plan," *CCC Mutual Monthly,* September–October 1925, 1.

30. Hennen, *Americanization of West Virginia,* 57–58.

31. Hennen, *Americanization of West Virginia;* Thomas, *Appalachian New Deal.*

32. Love, *Exciting Century,* 13–14; Hennen, *Americanization of West Virginia;* Salstrom, *Appalachia's Path to Dependency,* 89; Thomas, *Appalachian New Deal,* 98, 237.

33. Thomas, *Appalachian New Deal,* 8–9, 27.

34. *CCC Mutual Monthly,* July–August 1921, 47; November 1922, 15, 27, 30; December–January 1922–23, 31, 62; March 1923, 14; "Stay Put—It Pays," *CCC Mutual Monthly,* July–August 1925, 10.

35. "Thanksgiving," *CCC Mutual Monthly,* November 1921, 8; "The Dying Year," *CCC Mutual Monthly,* December–January 1922–1923, 10; "The Coal Industry," *CCC Mutual Monthly,* July–August 1925, 1; *CCC Mutual Monthly,* November–December 1925, 23; "Past, Present and Future," *CCC Mutual Monthly,* November 1921, 3–4; A. B. McGary, "Employee Representation in Pennsylvania," *CCC Mutual Monthly,* May–June 1927, 5–7.

Chapter 5

1. Francaviglia, *Hard Places,* xvii; Sekula, "Photography between Labour and Capital," 204. For an in-depth analysis of the U.S. copper industry's struggle to maintain profitability in the face of a diminishing resource, see Gavin Bridge, "The Social Regulation of Resource Access and Environmental Impact: Production, Nature and Contradiction in the Copper Industry," *Geoforum* 31 (2000): 237–56.

2. Black, "Order of Nature," 284–85, 297; Nye, *Image Worlds.*

3. Sontag quoted in Tuan, "Sight and Pictures," 421.

4. Thomas H. Garver, "Serving Places," introduction to *Invisible New York: The Hidden Infrastructure of the City* by Stanley Greenberg (Baltimore: Johns Hopkins University Press, 1998), 4; Black, "Order of Nature," 291. With regard to this last point, consider the way photographs of surface-mined lands are utilized and interpreted in Harry Caudill, *My Land Is Dying* (New York: Dutton, 1973).

5. M.-L. Quinn, "Industry and Environment in the Appalachian Copper Basin, 1890–1930," *Technology and Culture* 34 (July 1993): 575–612.

6. Homer Aschmann, "The Natural History of a Mine," *Economic Geography* 46 (April 1970): 171–90; Marion Clawson, *America's Land and Its Uses* (Baltimore: Johns Hopkins University Press, 1972).

7. Weller, *Yesterday's People,* 15; Buckley, "Minerals into Merchandise"; Harry M. Caudill, *Night Comes to the Cumberlands: A Biography of a Depressed Area* (Boston:

Little, Brown, 1963); Wilma Dunaway, "Speculators and Settler Capitalists: Unthinking the Mythology about Appalachian Landholding, 1790–1860," in *Appalachia in the Making: The Mountain South in the Nineteenth Century,* ed. M. B. Pudup, D. B. Billings, and A. L. Waller (Chapel Hill: University of North Carolina Press, 1995), 50–75; Eller, *Miners, Millhands, and Mountaineers;* Gaventa, *Power and Powerlessness;* Kirby, *Rural Worlds Lost.*

8. *CCC Mutual Monthly,* July 1918, 40–41.

9. President's Appalachian Regional Commission, *Appalachia's Forest Resources— Timber, A Task Force Report on the Timber Resources of Appalachia* (Washington, D.C.: Government Printing Office, 1963), iii, 39. Culls are trees that fail to meet minimum merchantability standards because of crookedness, limbiness, heart rot, or some other defect.

10. Green, "Consolidation Coal Company," 20; George B. Sudworth, "The Forests of Allegany County," in *Maryland Geological Survey: Allegany County* (Baltimore: Johns Hopkins Press, 1900), 282; Smith, *Mining America,* 13.

11. Sudworth, "Forests of Allegany County," 277–78; Fred W. Besley, *The Forests of Allegany County* (Baltimore: Maryland State Board of Forestry, 1912), 15–16; Sherry H. Olson, *The Depletion Myth: A History of Railroad Use of Timber* (Cambridge, Mass.: Harvard University Press, 1971); Karl B. Raitz and Richard Ulack, *Appalachia, A Regional Geography: Land, People, and Development* (Boulder: Westview Press, 1984); Nelson Courtlandt Brown, *Forest Products, Their Manufacture and Use: Embracing the Principal Commercial Features in the Production, Manufacture, and Utilization of the Most Important Forest Products Other than Lumber in the United States,* 2d ed. (New York: Wiley, 1927).

12. Roy B. Clarkson, *Tumult on the Mountain: Lumbering in West Virginia, 1770–1920* (Parsons, W.V.: McClain Printing Company, 1964); Eller, *Miners, Millhands, and Mountaineers;* Benjamin F. G. Kline Jr., *Tall Pines and Winding Rivers: The Logging Railroads of Maryland* (Lancaster, Pa.: B. F. G. Kline Jr., 1976); R. Lewis, *Transforming the Appalachian Countryside;* "Saw Mills in the Elkhorn Division," *CCC Mutual Monthly,* November 1918, 31.

13. "Saving Mine Timbers: Authorities Explain Best Methods for Preservation," *CCC Mutual Monthly,* May–June 1928, 33–34.

14. Ibid.

15. Sudworth, "Forests of Allegany County," 282. In this same report, Sudworth singles out the Consolidation Coal Company's efforts to use timber resources more wisely: "With scarcely an exception, the exploitation of tan-bark in the past was attended by a total waste of the timber, and most of the bark peeling of the present time leaves the trunks unused. The only exception observed by the writer was in recent work on the lands of the Consolidation Coal Company in the western part of the county. Here all peeled Chestnut Oak is being sawed up for mining timber with the other timber stripped from coal-bearing land" (277–78).

16. Luther Burbank, "Tree Planting," *CCC Mutual Monthly,* May–June 1928, 6.

17. William B. Clark and Edward B. Mathews, *Report on the Physical Features of Maryland, Together with an Account of the Exhibits of Maryland Mineral Resources Made by the Maryland Geological Survey* (Baltimore: Johns Hopkins Press, 1906); Fred W. Besley, *Maryland's Forest Resources: A Preliminary Report,* Forestry Leaflet

no. 7 (Baltimore: Maryland State Board of Forestry, 1909); Jillson, *Topography of Kentucky*, 238–39.

18. Jillson, *Topography of Kentucky*, 238–39. See also I. C. White, *Levels: Coal Analyses*, West Virginia Geological Survey Bulletin no. 2 (Morgantown: Acme Publishing Company, 1910).

19. Peter Roberts, *Anthracite Coal Communities: A Study of the Demography, the Social, Educational and Moral Life of the Anthracite Regions* (New York: Macmillan, 1904), 6.

20. Gordon A. Robb and James D. F. Robinson, "Acid Drainage from Mines," *Geographical Journal* 161 (March 1995): 47–54; John Uram and John E. Benhart, "Coal as a Natural Resource—the Long-Term Environmental Impacts: A Case Study of Carbondale, Pennsylvania," *Pennsylvania Geographer* 34 (Spring/Summer 1996): 40.

21. Jeanne M. Cordts, "The Hoffman Drainage Tunnel: A Remarkable Underground Achievement," *Journal of the Alleghenies* 13 (1977): 4, 6; *CCC Mutual Monthly*, October 1918, 28.

22. *Pennsylvania Coal Co. v. Sanderson*, 113 Pa. 126, 6 A. 453 (1886); William J. Gerlach, "Mine Drainage Liability in Pennsylvania Law" (Department of Environmental Protection, Bureau of Regulatory Counsel, unpublished).

23. Christine M. Rosen, "Costs and Benefits of Pollution Control in Pennsylvania, New York, and New Jersey, 1840–1906," *Geographical Review* 88 (April 1998): 219–40. In reference to a similar case that was playing out in Maryland, a column in the *Cumberland Evening Times* from 15 April 1905 stated, "There is . . . apparently no redress in the case of this pollution because of the fact that mine water is a necessary consequence of the development of coal regions. A precedent in the case of coal mine waste has been established by the supreme court of Pennsylvania, which held that as the contaminating material is a natural product and conducted into the stream in its natural state, mine operators are immune from injunction or damages."

24. Buckley, "Minerals into Merchandise"; Buckley, "Environmental Transformation"; U.S. Department of the Interior, *Drainage Basin of the Potomac*, 55th Cong., 2d sess., S. Doc. 90 (Washington, D.C.: Government Printing Office, 1898).

25. Roberts, *Anthracite Coal Communities*, 7.

26. *CCC Mutual Monthly*, May–June 1925, 23; November–December 1925, 26.

27. D. J. Cuff, W. J. Young, E. K. Muller, W. Zelinsky, and R. F. Abler, *The Atlas of Pennsylvania* (Philadelphia: Temple University Press, 1989).

28. Zegeer, "Mechanization of Appalachia's Coal Industry"; W. R. King, *The Surface Waters of Kentucky* (Frankfort: Kentucky Geological Survey, 1924), 10–11.

29. Consolidation Coal Company, *History*, 5; Black, "Order of Nature," 281.

30. Stephen Q. Hayes, "West Virginia's Opportunities," *CCC Mutual Monthly*, March 1924, 4; "West Virginia," *CCC Mutual Monthly*, March–April 1925, 26.

31. Kirby, *Rural Worlds Lost;* Thomas, *Appalachian New Deal*, 26.

Chapter 6

1. Sekula, "Photography between Labour and Capital," 195–97.

2. "Tipple at Mine No. 40 W. Va. Div.," *CCC Mutual Monthly*, November 1918, 73.

3. Paul J. Nyden, "Environmental Threats in Appalachia" in *Appalachia: Social Context Past and Present*, ed. Bruce Ergood and Bruce E. Kuhre, 3d ed. (Dubuque:

Kendall/Hunt Publishing, 1991), 243; Black, "Order of Nature," 284; Francaviglia, *Hard Places*, 215. As Williams and Muir show, there are many parallels between the photographs Consol took and the ones other large corporations took: "At first, photos were used for internal company information, but as the new technology for printing photographs developed, they were used increasingly for getting the DuPont Company message to the public." In time, photographs would be used by the company's sales department to illustrate their products and to publish in proceedings. They were also used for surveying purposes and to mark construction progress for various projects. Beginning in 1913, they were featured in *DuPont Magazine*. Williams and Muir, *Corporate Images*, 27–29.

   4. Nye, *Image Worlds*, 16; Williams and Muir, *Corporate Images*, 11. Photographs and text were on display on the front page of the Ashland *Daily Independent* for Friday, 15 September 1913. On that day, the newspaper carried the banner headline: "Jenkins–A Modern City in the Mountains and Newly Found Capital of an Inland Empire." Comparing the work that was being carried out in the coalfields of eastern Kentucky with the construction of the Panama Canal, the newspaper proclaimed that a model town was being constructed.

   5. Graebner, *Coal-Mining Safety*, 146–47; CCC *Mutual Monthly*, November–December 1926, 62–63.

   6. Meinig, "Beholding Eye," 42.

   7. Hennen, *Americanization of West Virginia*, xv; Corbin, *Life, Work, and Rebellion*, 123–24.

   8. Schein, "Representing Urban America," 14.

   9. Thomas, *Appalachian New Deal*, 18–19; Carol A. B. Giesen, *Coal Miners' Wives: Portraits of Endurance* (Lexington: University Press of Kentucky, 1995), 11.

   10. Kemp, *Lewis Hine*.

   11. Armstead, *Black Days*, 19; Merchant, *American Environmental History*.

   12. Schwartz, "'We Make Our Tools,'" 53. As Gillian Rose points out, the study of historical photograph collections should also cause us to examine the relationship between the researcher and the archive. Rose, "Practising Photography: An Archive, a Study, Some Photographs and a Researcher." *Journal of Historical Geography* 26 (October 2000): 555–71.

   13. Jack Owens, "Hollow Journey," *Now and Then*, Winter 2001, 11.

Bibliography

Books and Articles

Abramson, Rudy. "Mountaintop Removal: Necessity or Nightmare?" *Now and Then,* Winter 2001, 20–24.

Alanen, Arnold R. "The 'Locations': Company Communities on Minnesota's Iron Ranges." *Minnesota History* 48 (Fall 1982): 94–107.

Aldrich, Mark. "Preventing 'the Needless Peril of the Coal Mine': The Bureau of Mines and the Campaign against Coal Mine Explosions, 1910–1940." *Technology and Culture* (1995): 483–518.

Alexander, Toni. "The Deceptive Landscape: A Study in Ethnicity in Hornitos, California, 1860–1900." *California Geographer* 42 (2002): 41–59.

Allen, James B. *The Company Town in the American West.* Norman: University of Oklahoma Press, 1966.

Amundson, Michael A. "Home on the Range No More: The Boom and Bust of a Wyoming Uranium Mining Town, 1957–1988." *Western Historical Quarterly* 26 (4) (1995): 483–505.

Armstead, Robert. *Black Days, Black Dust: The Memories of an African American Coal Miner.* Knoxville: University of Tennessee Press, 2002.

Aschmann, Homer. "The Natural History of a Mine." *Economic Geography* 46 (April 1970): 171–90.

Banks, Alan. "Class Formation in the Southeastern Kentucky Coalfields, 1890–1920." In *Appalachia in the Making: The Mountain South in the Nineteenth Century,* ed. Mary Beth Pudup, Dwight B. Billings, and Altina L. Waller, 321–46. Chapel Hill: University of North Carolina Press, 1995.

———. "Miners Talk Back: Labor Activism in Southeastern Kentucky in 1922." In *Confronting Appalachian Stereotypes: Back Talk from an American Region,* ed. Dwight B. Billings, Gurney Norman, and Katherine Ledford. Lexington: University Press of Kentucky, 1999, 215–27.

Batteau, Allen W. *The Invention of Appalachia.* Tucson: University of Arizona Press, 1990.

Berger, John. "Understanding the Photograph." In *Classic Essays on Photography,* ed. Alan Trachtenberg, 292. New Haven: Leete's Island Books, 1980.

Billington, Ray A. "The Origin of the Speculator as a Frontier Type." *Agricultural History* 19 (October 1945): 204–12.

Black, Brian. "Petrolia: A Sacrificial Landscape of American Industrialization." *Landscape* 32 (2) (1994): 42–48.

———. "Recasting the Unalterable Order of Nature: Photography and the First Oil Boom." *Pennsylvania History: A Journal of Mid-Atlantic Studies* 64 (Spring 1997): 275–99.

Boyer, Peter J. "Rescue at Quecreek: An Accident and Its Consequences." *New Yorker,* 18 November 2002, 56–73.

Brannan, Beverly W., and David Horvath, eds. *A Kentucky Album: Farm Security Administration Photographs, 1935–1943*. Lexington: University Press of Kentucky, 1986.

Bridge, Gavin. "The Social Regulation of Resource Access and Environmental Impact: Production, Nature and Contradiction in the Copper Industry." *Geoforum* 31 (2000): 237–56.

Brown, Nelson Courtlandt. *Forest Products, Their Manufacture and Use: Embracing the Principal Commercial Features in the Production, Manufacture, and Utilization of the Most Important Forest Products Other than Lumber in the United States,* 2d ed. New York: Wiley, 1927.

Buckley, Geoffrey L. "Converting Minerals into Merchandise: Landownership and Environmental Alteration in the George's Creek Valley of Western Maryland, 1789–1842." *Historical Geography* 26 (1998): 151–75.

———. "The Environmental Transformation of an Appalachian Valley, 1850–1906." *Geographical Review* 88 (April 1998): 175–98.

Buckley, Geoffrey L., and Timothy G. Anderson. "The Consolidation Coal Company Photograph Collection, 1910–1945." *Appalachian Journal: A Regional Studies Review* 27 (Fall 1999): 62–83.

Buckley, Geoffrey L., and Betsy Burstein. "When Coal Was King: The Consolidation Coal Company's Maryland Division Photographs." *Maryland Historical Magazine* 91 (Fall 1996): 298–310.

Cable, Sherry. "From Fussin' to Organizing: Individual and Collective Resistance at Yellow Creek." In *Fighting Back in Appalachia: Traditions of Resistance and Change,* ed. Stephen L. Fisher, 69–83. Philadelphia: Temple University Press, 1993.

Caudill, Harry M. *My Land Is Dying.* New York: Dutton, 1973.

———. *Night Comes to the Cumberlands: A Biography of a Depressed Area.* Boston: Little, Brown, 1963.

———. *Theirs Be the Power: The Moguls of Eastern Kentucky.* Urbana: University of Illinois Press, 1983.

Clarkson, Roy B. *Tumult on the Mountain: Lumbering in West Virginia, 1770–1920.* Parsons, W.Va.: McClain Printing Company, 1964.

Clawson, Marion. *America's Land and Its Uses.* Baltimore: Johns Hopkins University Press, 1972.

Corbin, David Alan. *Life, Work, and Rebellion in the Coal Fields: The Southern West Virginia Miners, 1880–1922.* Urbana: University of Illinois Press, 1981.

Cordts, Jeanne M. "The Hoffman Drainage Tunnel: A Remarkable Underground Achievement." *Journal of the Alleghenies* 13 (1977): 3–7.

Cosgrove, Denis. "Prospect, Perspective, and the Evolution of the Landscape Idea." In

Reading Human Geography: The Poetics and Politics of Inquiry, ed. Trevor Barnes and Derek Gregory, 324–42. London: Arnold, 1997.

———. *Social Formation and Symbolic Landscape*. London: Croom Helm, 1984.

Cosgrove, Denis, and Stephen Daniels, eds. *The Iconography of Landscape: Essays on the Symbolic Representation, Design and Use of Past Environments*. Cambridge: Cambridge University Press, 1988.

Cronon, William. "Comment: Cutting Loose or Running Aground." *Journal of American History* 20 (1): 38–43.

Cuff, David J., William J. Young, Edward K. Muller, Wilbur Zelinsky, and Ronald F. Abler. *The Atlas of Pennsylvania*. Philadelphia: Temple University Press, 1989.

Dean, D. M. "New Directions, 1800–1865." In *Allegany County, A History*, by Harry I. Stegmaier Jr. et al., 91–199. Parsons, W.Va.: McClain Printing Company, 1976.

Dilts, James D. *The Great Road: The Building of the Baltimore and Ohio, the Nation's First Railroad, 1828–1853*. Stanford: Stanford University Press, 1993.

Dix, Keith. *What's a Coal Miner to Do? The Mechanization of Coal Mining*. Pittsburgh: University of Pittsburgh Press, 1988.

Domosh, Mona. "Visual Texts in Historical Geography." *Historical Geography* 29 (2001): 68.

Drake, Richard B. *A History of Appalachia*. Lexington: University Press of Kentucky, 2001.

Dramcyzk, Elizabeth W. *The History of Jenkins, Kentucky, Compiled in Honor of the Sixtieth Anniversary Homecoming Celebration, 1912–1973*. Sponsored by Jenkins Area Jaycees.

Drury, Doris. *The Accident Records in Coal Mines of the United States: A Study of the Literature with Comparisons of the Records in Other Coal-Producing Countries*. Bloomington: Department of Economics, Indiana University, 1964.

Dunaway, Wilma. *The First American Frontier: Transition to Capitalism in Southern Appalachia, 1700–1860*. Chapel Hill: University of North Carolina Press, 1996.

———. "Speculators and Settler Capitalists: Unthinking the Mythology about Appalachian Landholding, 1790–1860." In *Appalachia in the Making: The Mountain South in the Nineteenth Century*, ed. M. B. Pudup, D. B. Billings, and A. L. Waller, 50–75. Chapel Hill: University of North Carolina Press, 1995.

Duncan, James, and Nancy Duncan, "(Re)reading the Landscape." *Environment and Planning D: Society and Space* 6 (1988): 117–26.

Edney, Matthew H. *Mapping an Empire: The Geographical Construction of British India, 1765–1843*. Chicago: University of Chicago Press, 1997.

Edwards, Susan H. "Ben Shahn: The Road South." *History of Photography* 19 (Spring 1995): 13–19.

Eller, Ronald D. *Miners, Millhands, and Mountaineers: Industrialization of the Appalachian South, 1880–1930*. Knoxville: University of Tennessee Press, 1982.

Ergood, Bruce, and Bruce E. Kuhre, eds. *Appalachia: Social Context Past and Present*, 3d ed. Dubuque: Kendall/Hunt Publishing, 1991.

Farley, Gary, and Bill J. Leonard. "Mountain Preachers, Mountain Ministers." In *Christianity in Appalachia: Profiles in Regional Pluralism*, ed. Bill J. Leonard, 153–64. Knoxville: University of Tennessee Press, 1999.

Fisher, Andrea. *Let Us Now Praise Famous Women: Women Photographers for the U.S. Government, 1935 to 1944.* London: Pandora, 1987.

Fleischhauer, Carl, and Beverly W. Brannan, eds. *Documenting America, 1935–1943, with Essays by Lawrence W. Levine and Alan Trachtenberg.* Berkeley: University of California Press, in association with Library of Congress, 1988.

Francaviglia, Richard V. *Hard Places: Reading the Landscape of America's Historic Mining Districts.* Iowa City: University of Iowa Press, 1991.

———. "Mining and Landscape Transformation." In *The American Environment: Interpretations of Past Geographies,* ed. Lary M. Dilsaver and Craig E. Colten, 89–114. Lanham, Md.: Rowman and Littlefield, 1992.

Garver, Thomas H. "Serving Places." Introduction to *Invisible New York: The Hidden Infrastructure of the City* by Stanley Greenberg, 3–7. Baltimore: Johns Hopkins University Press, 1998.

Gaventa, John. "The Political Economy of Land Tenure: Appalachia and the Southeast." In *Who Owns America? Social Conflict Over Property Rights,* ed. Harvey M. Jacobs, 227–44. Madison: University of Wisconsin Press, 1998.

———. *Power and Powerlessness, Quiescence and Rebellion in an Appalachian Valley.* Urbana: University of Illinois Press, 1980.

Giesen, Carol A. B. *Coal Miners' Wives: Portraits of Endurance.* Lexington: University Press of Kentucky, 1995.

Goodell, Jeff. "How Coal Got Its Glow Back." *New York Times Magazine,* 22 July 2001, 30–37, 44, 62–63.

Graebner, William. *Coal-Mining Safety in the Progressive Period: The Political Economy of Reform.* Lexington: University Press of Kentucky, 1976.

Green, C. L. "The Consolidation Coal Company." *C.C.C. Mutual Magazine,* September–October 1926, 19–26.

Hanna, Stephen P. "Representation and the Reproduction of Appalachian Space: A History of Contested Signs and Meanings." *Historical Geography* 28 (2000): 179–207.

Harley, J. B. "Maps, Knowledge, and Power." In *The Iconography of Landscape: Essays on the Symbolic Representation, Design and Use of Past Environments,* ed. Denis Cosgrove and Stephen Daniels, 277–312. Cambridge: Cambridge University Press, 1988.

Harris, Cole. "The Historical Mind and the Practice of Geography." In *Humanistic Geography: Prospects and Problems,* ed., David Ley and Marwyn S. Samuels, 123–37. London: Croom Helm, 1978.

Harvey, David. *The Condition of Postmodernity: An Enquiry into the Origins of Cultural Change.* Oxford: Basil Blackwell, 1989.

Harvey, Katherine A. *The Best-Dressed Miners: Life and Labor in the Maryland Coal Region, 1835–1910.* Ithaca: Cornell University Press, 1969.

———. "Building a Frontier Iron Works: Problems of Transport and Supply, 1837–1840." *Maryland Historical Magazine* 70 (Summer 1975): 149–66.

Hass, Frank. "The Explosion at Monongah Number Six and Monongah Number Eight Mines of the Fairmont Coal Company, December 6, 1907." Copy on file at Fairmont State College Library, Fairmont, W.Va.

Heat-Moon, William Least. *Blue Highways: A Journey into America.* Boston: Little, Brown, 1982.

Hennen, John C. *The Americanization of West Virginia: Creating a Modern Industrial State, 1916–1925.* Lexington: University Press of Kentucky, 1996.

Hoelscher, Steven. "The Photographic Construction of Tourist Space in Victorian America." *Geographical Review* 88 (October 1998): 548–70.

Holdsworth, Deryck W. "Landscape and Archives as Texts." In *Understanding Ordinary Landscapes,* ed. Paul Groth and Todd W. Bressi, 44–55. New Haven: Yale University Press, 1997.

Hurley, F. Jack. "The Farm Security Administration File: In and Out of Focus." *History of Photography* 17 (Autumn 1993): 244–52.

Johnson, Brooks, ed. *Mountaineers to Main Streets: The Old Dominion Seen through the Farm Security Administration Photographs.* Norfolk: Chrysler Museum, 1985.

Kemp, John R., ed. *Lewis Hine: Photographs of Child Labor in the New South.* Jackson: University Press of Mississippi, 1986.

Kershaw, G. E. "Allegany County: The Frontier Years." In *Allegany County, A History,* by Harry I. Stegmaier Jr. et al., 3–56. Parsons, W.Va.: McClain Printing Company, 1976.

Kirby, Jack Temple. *Rural Worlds Lost: The American South, 1920–1960.* Baton Rouge: Louisiana State University Press, 1987.

Kline, Benjamin F. G., Jr. *Tall Pines and Winding Rivers: The Logging Railroads of Maryland.* Lancaster, Pa.: B. F. G. Kline Jr., 1976.

Land, Aubrey C. "A Land Speculator in the Opening of Western Maryland." *Maryland Historical Magazine* 48 (3) (1953): 191–203.

Larson, John Lauritz. *Bonds of Enterprise: John Murray Forbes and Western Development in America's Railway Age.* Boston: Harvard University Press, 1984.

Lewis, Peirce F. "Axioms for Reading the Landscape: Some Guides to the American Scene." In *The Interpretation of Ordinary Landscapes: Geographical Essays,* ed. Donald W. Meinig, 11–32. New York: Oxford University Press, 1979.

———. "The Monument and the Bungalow." *Geographical Review* 88 (October 1998): 507–27.

Lewis, Ronald L. "Appalachian Restructuring in Historical Perspective: Coal, Culture and Social Change in West Virginia." *Urban Studies* 30 (2) (1993): 299–308.

———. *Black Coal Miners in America: Race, Class, and Community Conflict, 1780–1980.* Lexington: University Press of Kentucky, 1987.

———. "From Peasant to Proletarian: The Migration of Southern Blacks to the Central Appalachian Coalfields." *Journal of Southern History* 55 (February 1989): 77–102.

———. *Transforming the Appalachian Countryside: Railroads, Deforestation, and Social Change in West Virginia, 1880–1920.* Chapel Hill: University of North Carolina Press, 1998.

Lowenthal, David. *The Past Is a Foreign Country.* Cambridge: Cambridge University Press, 1985.

Lutz, Catherine A., and Jane L. Collins. *Reading* National Geographic. Chicago: University of Chicago Press, 1993.

Lyell, Charles. *Travels in North America: With Geological Observations on the United States, Canada, and Nova Scotia.* London: J. Murray, 1845.

Marien, Mary Warner. *Photography and Its Critics: A Cultural History, 1839–1900.* Cambridge: Cambridge University Press, 1993.

McEuen, Melissa A. "Doris Ulmann and Marion Post Wolcott: The Appalachian South." *History of Photography* 19 (Spring 1995): 4–12.

Meinig, Donald W. "The Beholding Eye: Ten Versions of the Same Scene." In *The Interpretation of Ordinary Landscapes: Geographical Essays,* ed. Donald W. Meinig, 33–48. New York: Oxford University Press, 1979.

Mellander, Deane. *The Cumberland and Pennsylvania Railroad: Western Maryland's Historic Coal Carrier.* Newton, N.J.: Carstens Publications, 1981.

Melzer, Richard. "A Death in Dawson: The Demise of a Southwestern Company Town." *New Mexico Historical Review* 55 (4) (1980): 309–30.

Merchant, Carolyn. *The Columbia Guide to American Environmental History.* New York: Columbia University Press, 2002.

Mitchell, Don. *Cultural Geography: A Critical Introduction.* Oxford: Blackwell Publishers, 2000.

Mitchell, Robert D. *Commercialism and Frontier: Perspectives on the Early Shenandoah Valley.* Charlottesville: University Press of Virginia, 1977.

Mould, David H. "The Company Town That Outlived the Company: Haydenville, Ohio." *Journal of Cultural Geography* 5 (Spring/Summer 1985): 71–86.

Mulrooney, Margaret M. "A Legacy of Coal: The Coal Company Towns of Southwestern Pennsylvania." In *Perspectives in Vernacular Architecture,* IV, ed. Thomas Carter and Bernard L. Herman, 130–37. Columbia: University of Missouri, 1991.

Nevins, Allan, and Henry Steele Commager. *A Short History of the United States.* New York: Random House, 1945.

Nyden, Paul J. "Environmental Threats in Appalachia." In *Appalachia: Social Context Past and Present,* ed. Bruce Ergood and Bruce E. Kuhre, 243–53. 3d ed. Dubuque: Kendall/Hunt Publishing, 1991.

Nye, David E. *Image Worlds: Corporate Identities at General Electric, 1890–1930.* Cambridge, Mass.: MIT Press, 1985.

Olson, Sherry H. *The Depletion Myth: A History of Railroad Use of Timber.* Cambridge, Mass.: Harvard University Press, 1971.

Owens, Jack. "Hollow Journey." *Now and Then* (Winter 2001): 11–14.

"Proud to Be a Miner." *United Mine Workers Journal: A Special Bicentennial Issue,* 15 July 1976.

Purdy, Jedediah S. "Rape of the Appalachians." In *Appalachia: Social Context Past and Present,* ed. Phillip J. Obermiller and Michael E. Maloney, 208–14. Dubuque: Kendall/Hunt Publishing Company, 2002.

Quinn, M.-L. "Industry and Environment in the Appalachian Copper Basin, 1890–1930." *Technology and Culture* 34 (July 1993): 575–612.

Raitz, Karl B., and Richard Ulack. *Appalachia, A Regional Geography: Land, People, and Development.* Boulder: Westview Press, 1984.

Rasmussen, Barbara. *Absentee Landownership and Exploitation in West Virginia, 1760–1920.* Lexington: University of Kentucky Press, 1994.

Ray, R. Glenn. "Portal to Portal: My Experience Mining Coal in Ohio." *Appalachian Journal: A Regional Studies Review* 21 (Fall 1993): 24–49.

Reizenstein, Milton. *The Economic History of the Baltimore and Ohio Railroad, 1827–1853.* Baltimore: Johns Hopkins Press, 1897.

Relph, Edward. *The Modern Urban Landscape.* Baltimore: Johns Hopkins University Press, 1987.

————. *Rational Landscapes and Humanistic Geography*. London: Croom Helm, 1981.

Reps, John W. *Bird's Eye Views: Historic Lithographs of North American Cities*. New York: Princeton Architectural Press, 1998.

————. *Cities on Stone: Nineteenth Century Lithograph Images of the Urban West*. Fort Worth: Amon Carter Museum, 1976.

Ritchin, Fred. *In Our Own Image: The Coming Revolution in Photography*. New York: Aperture, 1990.

Robb, Gordon A., and James D. F. Robinson. "Acid Drainage from Mines." *Geographical Journal* 161 (March 1995): 47–54.

Roberts, Peter. *Anthracite Coal Communities: A Study of the Demography, the Social, Educational and Moral Life of the Anthracite Regions*. New York: Macmillan, 1904.

Rose, Gillian. "Practising Photography: An Archive, a Study, Some Photographs and a Researcher." *Journal of Historical Geography* 26 (October 2000): 555–71.

Rosen, Christine M. "Costs and Benefits of Pollution Control in Pennsylvania, New York, and New Jersey, 1840–1906." *Geographical Review* 88 (April 1998): 219–40.

Rosler, Martha. "In, Around, and Afterthoughts (on Documentary Photography)." In *The Context of Meaning: Critical Histories of Photography*. Cambridge, Mass.: MIT Press, 1989.

Rundell, Walter, Jr. *Early Texas Oil*. College Station: Texas A&M University Press, 1977.

Salstrom, Paul. *Appalachia's Path to Dependency: Rethinking a Region's Economic History, 1730–1940*. Lexington: University Press of Kentucky, 1994.

Salstrom, Paul, and Steve Hollenhorst. "Increasing Dependency and the Touristization Rag." *Appalachian Journal* 21 (Summer 1994): 410–20.

Scharf, J. Thomas. *History of Western Maryland*. 1882. Reprint, Baltimore: Regional Publishing Company, 1968.

Schein, Richard H. "The Place of Landscape: A Conceptual Framework for Interpreting an American Scene." *Annals of the Association of American Geographers* 87 (4) (1997): 660–80.

————. "Representing Urban America: Nineteenth-Century Views of Landscape, Space, and Power." *Environment and Planning D: Society and Space* 11 (1993): 7–21.

Schwantes, Carlos A. *Vision and Enterprise: Exploring the History of Phelps Dodge Corporation*. Tucson: University of Arizona Press: 2000.

Schwartz, Joan M. "*The Geography Lesson:* Photographs and the Construction of Imaginative Geographies." *Journal of Historical Geography* 22 (1) (1996): 16–45.

————. "'Records of Simple Truth and Precision': Photography, Archives, and the Illusion of Control." *Archivaria* 50 (Fall 2000): 1–40.

————. "'We Make Our Tools and Our Tools Make Us': Lessons from Photographs for the Practice, Politics, and Poetics of Diplomatics." *Archivaria* 40 (Fall 1995): 40–74.

Sekula, Allan. "Photography between Labour and Capital." In *Mining Photographs and Other Pictures: A Selection from the Negative Archives of Shedden Studio, Glace Bay, Cape Breton, 1948–1968,* ed. Benjamin H. D. Buchloh and Robert Wilkie, 192–268. Halifax: Press of the Nova Scotia College of Art and Design, 1983.

Shifflett, Crandall A. *Coal Towns: Life, Work, and Culture in Company Towns of Southern Appalachia, 1880–1960.* Knoxville: University of Tennessee Press, 1991.
———. "Coaltowns: The Company Town and Southern Appalachian History." In *Appalachia: Social Context Past and Present,* ed. Bruce Ergood and Bruce E. Kuhre, 3d ed., 194–97. Dubuque: Kendall/Hunt Publishing, 1991.

Smith, Duane A. *Mining America: The Industry and the Environment, 1800–1980.* Niwot, Colo.: University Press of Colorado, 1993.

Snyder, Robert E. "Photography and the American South: A Bibliographical Introduction." *History of Photography* 19 (Spring 1995): 1–3.

Sontag, Susan. "Looking at War: Photography's View of Devastation and Death." *New Yorker,* 9 December 2002, 82–98.

Stange, Maren. "Documentary Photography in American Social Reform: The FSA Project and Its Predecessors." In *Multiple Views: Logan Grant Essays on Photography, 1983–1989,* ed. Daniel P. Younger, 195–223. Albuquerque: University of New Mexico Press, 1991.

Stover, John F. *History of the Baltimore and Ohio Railroad.* West Lafayette, Ind.: Purdue University Press, 1987.

Thomas, Jerry Bruce. *An Appalachian New Deal: West Virginia in the Great Depression.* Lexington: University Press of Kentucky, 1998.

Trachtenberg, Alan. "From Image to Story: Reading the File." In *Documenting America, 1935–1943,* ed. Carl Fleischhauer and Beverly W. Brannan, 43–73. Berkeley: University of California Press, in association with the Library of Congress, 1988.
———. *Reading American Photographs: Images as History, Mathew Brady to Walker Evans.* New York: Hill and Wang, 1989.

Tuan, Yi-Fu. "Sight and Pictures." *Geographical Review* 69 (October 1979): 413–22.
———. "Thought and Landscape: The Eye and the Mind's Eye." In *The Interpretation of Ordinary Landscapes: Geographical Essays,* ed. Donald W. Meinig, 89–102. New York: Oxford University Press, 1979.

Uram, John, and John E. Benhart. "Coal as a Natural Resource—the Long-Term Environmental Impacts: A Case Study of Carbondale, Pennsylvania." *Pennsylvania Geographer* 34 (Spring/Summer 1996): 38–63.

Wallach, Bret. *At Odds with Progress.* Tucson: University of Arizona Press, 1991.

Ward, Geoffrey C. *Before the Trumpet: Young Franklin Roosevelt, 1882–1905.* New York: Harper and Row, 1985.

Ware, Donna M. *Green Glades and Sooty Gob Piles: The Maryland Coal Region's Industrial and Architectural Past.* Crownsville: Maryland Historical and Cultural Publications, 1995.
———. "Rails, Resources, and Resorts: The Opening of Maryland's Coal Region." *Maryland Humanities* (Spring/Summer 1995): 11–13.

Weiss, Margaret R. *Ben Shahn, Photographer: An Album from the Thirties.* New York: Da Capo Press, 1973.

Weller, Jack E. *Yesterday's People: Life in Contemporary Appalachia.* Lexington: University Press of Kentucky, 1965.

Williams, John Alexander. *West Virginia and the Captains of Industry.* Morgantown: West Virginia University Foundation, 1976.

Williams, Jon M., and Daniel T. Muir, *Corporate Images: Photography and the DuPont Company, 1865–1972*. Wilmington, Del.: Hagley Museum and Library, 1984.

Wiseman, John B. "The Whirligig of Change, 1865–1920." In *Allegany County, A History*, by Harry I. Stegmaier Jr. et al., 201–97. Parsons, W.Va.: McClain Printing Company, 1976.

Wyckoff, William, and Lary M. Dilsaver. "Promotional Imagery of Glacier National Park." *Geographical Review* 87 (January 1997): 1–26.

Zegeer, David A. "The Mechanization of Appalachia's Coal Industry: Consolidation Coal and Town of Jenkins Led the Way." *Kentucky Explorer* 16 (9) (2002): 10–14.

Newspapers and Magazines

Ashland (Ky.) Daily Independent
The Check Board (1947)
Consolidation Coal Company Mutual Monthly Magazine (1918–28)
Consol News (1962–72)
Cumberland (Md.) Alleganian
Cumberland Daily Times
Cumberland Sunday Times
Cumberland Union and Allegany County Gazette
Fairmont (W.Va.) Free Press
New York Times
Washington Post

Industry Records and Publications

Beachley, Charles E. *History of the Consolidation Coal Company, 1864–1934.* New York: Consolidation Coal Company, 1934.

Christiansen, A. J. *Production of Coal: Bituminous and Anthracite, Years 1800 to 1947 by States and Producing Districts and the United States.* Chicago: Northern Illinois Coal Trade Association, 1948.

"The Coal Field of Allegany County, Maryland." *National Magazine and Industrial Record* 1 (October 1845): 431–43.

Consolidation Coal Company. *A History of Consolidation Coal Company.* Pittsburgh: Consolidation Coal Company, Public Relations Department, 1989.

Harvey, Katherine A., ed. "The Lonaconing Journals: The Founding of a Coal and Iron Community, 1837–1840." *Transactions of the American Philosophical Society* 67, pt. 2. Philadelphia: American Philosophical Society, 1977.

Hughes, George W. *Excerpts from Reports of an Examination of the Coal Measures Belonging to the Maryland Mining Company in Allegany County and of a Survey for a Railroad from the Mines to the Chesapeake and Ohio Canal, at Cumberland.* Washington, D.C.: Printed by Gales and Seaton, 1837.

Love, George H. *An Exciting Century in Coal, 1864–1964* Address given by the president of the Pittsburgh Consolidation Coal Company at Pittsburgh. New York: Newcomen Society in North America, 1955.

Nicolls, William Jasper. *Above Ground and Below in the George's Creek Coal Region.* Baltimore: Consolidation Coal Company, 1898.

Robbins, W. B. *Cheap Fuel.* Louisville: Kentucky Fuel Company, 1 November 1855.

Silliman, Benjamin. *Extracts from a report made to the Maryland and New York Coal & Iron Company on the estate of said company, in the county of Alleghany [sic], state of Maryland.* London: Printed by T. C. Savill, 1839.

———. *Extracts from a report made to the Maryland Mining Company on the estate of said company, in the county of Allegany, Maryland.* New York: Printed by Scatcherd and Adams, 1838.

Government Documents

Besley, Fred W. *The Forests of Allegany County.* Baltimore: Maryland State Board of Forestry, 1912.

———. *Maryland's Forest Resources: A Preliminary Report.* Forestry Leaflet no. 7. Baltimore: Maryland State Board of Forestry, 1909.

Clark, William Bullock. *Maryland Geological Survey: Report on the Coals of Maryland.* Baltimore: Johns Hopkins Press, 1905.

Clark, William B., and Edward B. Mathews. *Report on the Physical Features of Maryland, Together with an Account of the Exhibits of Maryland Mineral Resources Made by the Maryland Geological Survey.* Baltimore: Johns Hopkins Press, 1906.

Collins, Timothy, Ronald D. Eller, and Glen Edward Taul. *Kentucky River Area Development District: Historical Trends and Geographic Patterns.* Lexington: University of Kentucky, Appalachian Center, 1996.

Crowell, Douglas L. *History of the Coal-Mining Industry in Ohio.* Bulletin no. 72. Columbus: Ohio Department of Natural Resources, Division of Geological Survey, 1995.

Gerlach, William J. "Mine Drainage Liability in Pennsylvania Law." (Department of Environmental Protection, Bureau of Regulatory Counsel, unpublished.)

Jillson, Willard Rouse. *The Topography of Kentucky.* Frankfort: Kentucky Geological Survey, 1927.

King, W. R. *The Surface Waters of Kentucky.* Frankfort: Kentucky Geological Survey, 1924.

Lacoste, K. C., and R. D. Wall. *An Archaeological Study of the Western Maryland Coal Region: The Historic Resources.* Baltimore: Maryland Geological Survey, 1987.

"Map of Military Lots, Tracts, Escheats, &c. in Garrett County, MD and Allegany County, MD West of Cumberland. Prepared Under Act of 1874 Chapter 322 &c. Scale: 200 Perches to 1 Inch." Copy on file at Maryland State Archives, Annapolis.

National Research Council. Committee on Underground Coal Mine Safety. *Toward Safer Underground Coal Mines.* Washington, D.C.: National Academy Press, 1982.

President's Appalachian Regional Commission, *Appalachia's Forest Resources—Timber, A Task Force Report on the Timber Resources of Appalachia.* Washington, D.C.: Government Printing Office, 1963.

Smithsonian Institution, National Museum of American History. "A Guide to the Collection: The Pittsburgh Consolidation Coal Company Records, Consolidation Coal Company Photographs." Washington, D.C.: unpublished, 28 November 2000.

Sudworth, George B. "The Forests of Allegany County." In *Maryland Geological Survey: Allegany County*. Baltimore: Johns Hopkins Press, 1900.

U.S. Department of the Interior. *Drainage Basin of the Potomac*, 55th Cong., 2d sess., S. Doc. 90. Washington, D.C.: Government Printing Office, 1898.

White, I. C. *Levels: Coal Analyses*. West Virginia Geological Survey Bulletin no. 2. Morgantown: Acme Publishing Company, 1910.

Index